ALIVE

in the

SPIRIT

CLIVE CALVER

Charisma
HOUSE
A STRANG COMPANY

Most Strang Communications/Charisma House/Siloam products are available at special quantity discounts for bulk purchase for sales promotions, premiums, fund-raising, and educational needs. For details, write Strang Communications/Charisma House/Siloam, 600 Rinehart Road, Lake Mary, Florida 32746, or telephone (407) 333-0600.

Alive in the Spirit by Clive Calver
Published by Charisma House
A Strang Company
600 Rinehart Road
Lake Mary, Florida 32746
www.charismahouse.com

Unless otherwise noted, all Scripture quotations are from the Holy Bible, New International Version. Copyright © 1973, 1978, 1984, International Bible Society. Used by permission.

Scripture quotations marked GNT are from the *Good News Translation*, second edition, copyright © 1992 by American Bible Society. Used by permission.

Scripture quotations marked KJV are from the King James Version of the Bible.

Scripture quotations marked NKJV are from the New King James Version of the Bible. Copyright © 1979, 1980, 1982 by Thomas Nelson, Inc., publishers. Used by permission.

Scripture quotations marked NLT are from the Holy Bible, New Living Translation, copyright © 1996. Used by permission of Tyndale House Publishers, Inc., Wheaton, IL, 60189. All rights reserved.

Scripture quotations marked RSV are from the Revised Standard Version of the Bible. Copyright © 1946, 1952, 1971 by the Division of Christian Education of the National Council of the Churches of Christ in the USA. Used by permission.

Cover design by Judith McKittrick

Library of Congress Cataloging-in-Publication Data:
Calver, Clive.
  Alive in the spirit / Clive Calver.
    p. cm.
  ISBN 1-59185-872-0 (pbk.)
  1. Holy Spirit--Prayer-books and devotions--English. 2. Devotional calendars. I. Title.
  BT123.C34 2006
  231'.3--dc22
                            2005012290

First Edition

06 07 08 09 10 — 9 8 7 6 5 4 3 2 1
Printed in the United States of America

Dedication

THIS BOOK IS born out of a love for the church worldwide. It is designed to speak to both individuals and to congregations alike, to tell of the Holy Spirit who longs to work through our individual lives in order to make the church truly resemble its Lord and Founder, Jesus Christ.

It is dedicated to all those who have taught me to recognize the reality of the Holy Spirit.

Especially to Sam and Debbie, and all their team of African leaders, who seek to bring the power of the Holy Spirit to transform lives in Southern Africa.

And to our friends who worship at Walnut Hill, who through that same Holy Spirit continue to seek to make an impact for renewal in New England today.

ACKNOWLEDGMENTS

NO BOOK CAN ever be a completely solo project. Many are involved at various stages, and they should each receive their fair share of the credit. Any blame I will, of course, reserve for myself!

Having always believed that the role of the Holy Spirit is fundamental to our Christian lives, the first and second editions of *The Holy Spirit* were released in Britain. My desire to share the same thoughts in the United States resulted in a new edition being printed here titled *Descending Like a Dove*. However, it was still on my heart to produce a whole different project that would enable us, as individuals, to engage with the Holy Spirit daily. Therefore, this book is what I have chosen to term "a personal Pentecost project." It is my prayer that over the next fifty days, each reader will be able to understand and relate to the Holy Spirit in a deeper way, ultimately having a life-changing encounter with Him.

Even though I have lived in the United States for the last eight years, I still have a long way to go to assimilate all those cultural and linguistic differences that truly do combine to make us what that famous playwright George Bernard Shaw said: "two countries divided by a common language." So to the many who have helped in this book, either by featuring in these pages or contributing in other ways toward the book's production, please accept my grateful thanks.

I want to express my thanks to Stephen Strang, who has been a trusted friend over several years, and to all the staff of Strang Communications for believing that this book really does have a message today for the American church. My sincere appreciation and thanks go to Bert Ghezzi for his confidence in this project and his determination to see it through. I also want to thank all those who have translated my "Englishness," working to make this manuscript more relevant.

My thanks are therefore also due to the Board of World Relief for allowing me the time and opportunity to address this task and to Walnut Hill Community Church for their support and participation in this project.

Above all, I want to thank those who have been part of this book—and all the family and friends who have become involved at some point in the journey. Thank you to the many who have provided inspiration and support over the years and provided much of the content for this work.

Of course, Anne Calver, whose indefatigable efforts enabled the reformatting of an old manuscript to emerge into the book that it is today. Anne not only assisted in the manuscript, but she also provided the original material for the small study groups. For so much gifted hard work I am grateful—and proud—of my daughter-in-law for all her creative efforts.

Finally, I express my appreciation to you for being prepared to read, to share a dream and a prayer that the Holy Spirit might keep us moving on with Him into all that the future holds for the people of God. Finally, thank you to the Lord, Father, Son, and Holy Spirit, because in so many ways He has only made a beginning with each one of us, and by His grace there will be still many chapters left to write.

CONTENTS

WEEK FOUR
SUPERNATURAL LIVING

WEEK FIVE
GIFTS AND GRACES

WEEK SIX
SPIRIT-FILLED CHURCHES

WEEK SEVEN
LIVING BY THE SPIRIT

SMALL GROUP STUDY GUIDE

Introduction

EVERY BOOK IS designed to tell a story, but each one will employ different methods in order to make the story live for its readers. This particular book is no exception!

Following each daily entry is material for individual study that will expound on the material. These personal studies are provided to help each one of us to live as Jesus intended and to continue, therefore, developing our daily knowledge of, and encounter with, His Holy Spirit.

It may often be helpful to discuss and exchange views and experiences with others. That is why specially designed materials for small-group interaction are included at the back of the book.

Ultimately it is my prayer that the Lord will speak to each one of us during these fifty days of material that symbolize the period that the early church knew as Pentecost. For in fifty days the Lord Jesus transformed a bunch of cowering, frightened followers into those who were to turn their world upside down. He did it then in the power of His Holy Spirit, and He still does the same today.

What is required for this miracle to take place? The answer lies in part with our desire to know that God is at work in our hearts and lives. When this is revealed in an open and sensitive spirit that is waiting for God, and when it is demonstrated by a heart and mind that is prepared to pray and to learn, then the basic entrance requirements have been fulfilled. Who can guess at what God will do in fifty days?

Whether it is through the written material, the opportunity given for personal reflection, or in small-group discussion, I pray that we will receive all that the Lord wants to reveal to us. My desire is that the Holy Spirit will be given the position in our lives that He deserves and that each one of us will know the power of the Spirit at work in our lives in ways that perhaps we have never known before.

For God always desires to be at work among His people. He is at work within every one of us who have surrendered our lives to the Lord Jesus. That it is why this is so important. I strongly believe that the Lord wants to transform our ministries and to make us wonderfully effective for Him. But in order to do this, He wants us to grapple with our understanding of the Holy Spirit on our own and with one another. The Father's heart is to equip each one of us individually, and as a body, to recognize the importance of His Spirit's work in our lives. So during this period of fifty days it is worth investing time and prayer. The prayer of each of us involved in the production of this book is that, at the end, no one will still feel that he is not alive in the Spirit.

WEEK ONE

WHERE WOULD WE BE WITHOUT THE SPIRIT?

Though a man may know Greek and Hebrew fluently, and though he may have committed the Old and New Testaments to memory, and though he may know all the commentaries, if he is not filled with the Spirit, he cannot be a true guide to you in the things of God.

—CHUCK SMITH
THE SIGNS OF THE SPIRIT

DAY 1

THE BEGINNING:
Is Anyone Thirsty?

A CLOSE FRIEND was speaking to a group of Christian leaders at a large conference. He began to challenge them as to the role of the Holy Spirit within their church communities. He concluded, as many others have done, that if the Spirit were to be taken from us, 95 percent of our church activities would go on exactly as before. At the end of the session, a question was asked. One of the leaders wanted to know how to structure the local church so that the other 5 percent would be covered as well!

Where would we be without the Holy Spirit? This is one question that many of us can be too cautious to ask. We have seen and heard so much about those extremists who place the whole emphasis of their Christian lives upon this single issue. Furthermore, we may well dislike some of those television programs and events that we have viewed. Even worse, we may have experienced what it means to be personally exposed to specific situations where spiritual ministry appears to have been abused.

All of these can certainly explain the legitimate apprehension with which some of us may approach this crucial doctrine. We sense the need to avoid the dangers that could result from an overemphasis on this one subject and to be careful not to get carried away in a mere hunger for experience.

But for those who are passionately hungry for more of the reality of God in their lives, being frightened of becoming fanatics can never act as a sufficient deterrent. The fact is that a desire for a deeper and more intimate relationship with Him should ultimately surpass all of our deepest fears.

After all, it was the Lord Jesus Himself who said He would send His Spirit who would lead us into all truth. When we miss out on the Holy Spirit, we miss out on the spirit of Jesus at our own risk!

Then there are others who fall into a different kind of trap. For them the Holy Spirit is all about being relegated to their personal experience. This becomes the litmus test by which everybody is then judged, with the crucial question being, how far does our personal encounter with the Holy Spirit match up to theirs?

1

Neither extreme gives us the real solution, but does that invalidate the question? The answer is of course not. So where would we be, both individually and collectively, without the Holy Spirit? Sadly, in too many cases, and often for far too many of us, the truth is that we would be in exactly the same place as we are today!

HUNGRY FOR GOD

But the situation is not hopeless. One of the single most exciting things that I am discovering about life in the American church today is that a growing number of people are becoming dissatisfied. They are exhibiting distinct signs of frustration.

It is not that they are upset with Jesus or frustrated in their family or professional lives. Neither are they particularly uptight with the church. They are beginning to exhibit signs of a holy dissatisfaction with their current spiritual condition. They want to be able to precipitate change in this world, but they are not sure if they are capable of making a difference or even if they are worthy of being given the opportunity.

Many of us are willing to admit that we are hungry to know more of the reality of God in our daily lives, but we are not quite sure where to find answers to our problems or for our spiritual thirst to be quenched.

Now I believe that this is good news. Apathy and self-indulgence have come close to destroying spiritual vitality in Western Christendom over the last century or more. We have concentrated on all that we could get out of Jesus, when He has called us to build His kingdom rather than our own. He has called us to be holy, when we just wanted to be happy.

It seems that for too long we have appeared to be content with just going through the motions. We have performed our religious duties of church-going, praying, and reading our Bibles. But it has all been such a passive response to the crucified love that the Son of God had poured out for us.

We have been destined to make an impact upon our world. We were never designed to simply limp our way feebly through life, avoiding whatever pitfalls we could along the way, until we finally found ourselves in heaven. Instead we were made to pour our lives out in the service of the King who gave His life for us. Then finally we make our triumphant entrance into heaven secure in the knowledge that the Holy Spirit has been at work through our lives to transform a little of this world for Jesus Christ.

If we are not satisfied with what we have now and want to change this world for Jesus, then we might just be prepared to venture out into uncharted territory and trust that we will find God there.

This book is written for those of us who are asking the simple question: "But how?" The reply from heaven is unequivocal: "'Not by might nor by power, but by my Spirit' says the LORD Almighty" (Zech. 4:6).

It is not drifting along in our human energies and efforts. Nor is it by merely adopting a spiritual program that has worked for others and that we hope might work for us. But it is by searching for a deepening reality of God, the Holy Spirit, within each one of our lives.

THOUGHT FOR THE DAY

Come, all you who are thirsty, come to the waters; and you who have no money, come, buy and eat!

—ISAIAH 55:1

WAIT A MINUTE

Christ wants you to experience "resurrected" life through His Spirit living in you. In other words, His heart is for each one of us to know life in all its fullness.

If you are experiencing a lull in your life and a sense of dissatisfaction with the spiritual climate around you, it may be because the Spirit of God is creating a hunger in your heart for more of the reality of God. If this thirst is filling your soul and you don't know where to go for it to be quenched, begin to search for a deepening reality of the Holy Spirit in your life. Remember that He wants to give life to your mortal body by His Spirit, so if you ask Him to come, He *will* hear your cry.

QUESTIONS TO CONTEMPLATE

1. How thirsty are you for the Spirit?

2. Do you feel a desire burning in your heart for more?

SPACE TO REFLECT

The Lord wants you to come and take a drink today to give you a deeper sense of the reality of the Spirit at work in your life. Today marks the start of a new spiritual journey.

A TIME TO PRAY

Lord Almighty, thank You that what I see around me here on earth today is not all that there is. Thank You that there is so much more to knowing You. Lord, please quench my thirst for You. Please extend my understanding of You and give me fresh revelation of Your Spirit at work in and through my life. In Jesus' name, amen.

THE REALITY:
GOD IN US!

RHODA SITS ALONE each day in the dust and the dirt of the streets of Lilongwe, the capital city of the East African country of Malawi. Rhoda is blind, and no employer will adapt a job to suit her skills. So each day she begs, seeking enough money to eke out a frugal existence for herself and her mentally defective husband. His problems make it impossible for him to work, so their survival is dependent upon Rhoda.

Rhoda is a Christian. She is part of our worldwide family because, like us, she loves Jesus. As she leaves an unfurnished hovel she calls "home," Rhoda senses rather than sees people passing her by. A tiny, squawking bundle of fragile humanity clings to her. The child is not her own, but a granddaughter. Rhoda's own daughter died from AIDS when the child was only a few days old. Now the blind grandmother is the only one left to care for the baby, and the child is almost certainly infected with the HIV virus that must have been transmitted from the mother.

On the morning that my wife, Ruth, had met this poor blind lady, she had just discovered that her only earthly possession—a precious water jar—had been stolen from her side.

In her own inimitably, straightforward style, Ruth asked Rhoda a profound and significant question: "Do you have a message that you would like me to take back from Africa to your brothers and sisters in the West?"

Rhoda would have every human reason to feel resentful about the way that her life has turned out, but instead she instantly responded, "Yes, there is something that I would like you to tell them. I want you to pass along the message that Rhoda is doing well, and that all is fine for me here. Please say to my brothers and sisters that I have everything I could need, because I have Jesus!"

We may marvel at the simple faith of this saint of God. We may wonder how it is that someone who possesses so little materially has so much spiritually. We may question how it could be that someone who has been deprived of so much by the circumstances of life could somehow cling so tenaciously to the conviction that she is truly loved of God.

The answer is so simple and straightforward. The only credible explanation is that such faith is supernatural in origin and can only be accounted for as the work of the Holy Spirit. It would certainly take the provision of divine strength enabling Rhoda to exhibit such supreme faith and confidence in the presence and power of Jesus, which was so at work in her life.

The consistent demonstration of such dramatic qualities can ultimately originate only in the Holy Spirit Himself. Yet the painful reality in the life of too many churches in America today is that the Holy Spirit has too often received little or no acknowledgment at all. At times, He can almost appear to have been subconsciously excluded in our minds from the Godhead!

He has been called "the author of every positive revolution in the history of the church," "Satan's unsolved problem," or "God's secret weapon, bringing explosive life to His people." Now all of these may be accurate, but during whole chunks of Christian history the Holy Spirit has more often been regarded as the silent partner in Deity, the forgotten member of the Trinity.

This is a strange and unsatisfactory verdict on the one who, within the "Triune" Godhead, is the person who communicates the love and presence of God, and this is no mere external communication. For the Holy Spirit actually resides within the lives of those who have surrendered themselves to the forgiveness and saving love that has been brought to them by Jesus Christ.

THE GOD WHO COMES TO US!

Once an individual confesses his sins and rejection of God's love, then he can receive divine forgiveness, which is made possible by crucified love. For when Jesus died on the cross, He took all of our guilt, penalty, consequences, punishment, and alienation from Father God upon Himself. In this wonderful "atonement," He gave us a way back home and a new beginning that was unprecedented in human history. He gave us forgiveness, not just from our family and friends, but a divine forgiveness that wipes out all of our past guilt and sin. No wonder it became known as "good news"!

Then, in the light of our response of repentance and faith in Him and all that He has done for us, Jesus introduces us as new believers to His Father and into His family (Rom. 5:10). Then He puts His seal, not upon us, but *within* us!

The same Holy Spirit who was originally at work in drawing us to Christ is now placed by the Father and the Son within us as the seal of this new relationship (Rom. 5:5). This is to equip and enable us to live our new lives in the way that God intends (Rom. 8:13).

So the Holy Spirit comes to make everything new in the life of the believer. Only the Holy Spirit can do this, for He is God and living within each and every Christian (Rom. 8:13–14). Possibly the only appropriate response is to roar along with the angels in heaven the single word—*hallelujah!*

This same Holy Spirit represents just about the only feasible explanation for how Rhoda could face such adverse circumstances but could still live, against all the odds, a truly triumphant life in Jesus. For when our human nature is at a loss to cope or to know what to do, there are divine resources to draw on.

This offer of God living in us is one to which many, like Rhoda, have responded. God, far from being distant, now stays with us in the most intimate relationship possible. How is this possible?

In the final analysis, the Holy Spirit is no less than the reality of the very presence of the living God who is busy making His home in the life of every believer.

He is too important to miss out on!

THOUGHT FOR THE DAY

We have not received the spirit of the world but the Spirit who is from God, that we may understand what God has freely given us.
—1 CORINTHIANS 2:12

WAIT A MINUTE

The gift that Rhoda received from her Lord and King is the same special gift that we have graciously been given. The Holy Spirit dwelt in her life in such a real way that she had a unique and special relationship with Jesus. The Lord's heart is for us to know Him and His ways in a special unique way, too, and to realize the significance of the Spirit's power at work in us *today!*

It is tough for us to relate to the Malawian lady, especially surrounded by so much material wealth and prosperity. However, the Spirit still calls on us to draw strength from Him and to put all our confidence in Him, even over the small things. We do not just accept that Jesus has died and risen, but we need to accept the reality that His Spirit's seal has been put *within* each one of us. Therefore, if we were left with nothing, we would still have so much, because we would have our Lord and a real, tangible faith in Him.

QUESTIONS TO CONTEMPLATE

1. Do you think that the Holy Spirit is often a silent member of the Trinity in your life?

2. How can you esteem Him and His work in your life as highly as you value the Father and the Son?

SPACE TO REFLECT

Consider Rhoda's life. Perhaps there is something from her story that you can take away today in order to benefit your daily walk with the Lord.

A TIME TO PRAY

Lord, I praise You today that You live in me! Thank You that You did not just ascend to heaven leaving me alone on earth. Thank You that You sent Your Spirit to dwell in my life. I pray that I will never allow Him to be the forgotten member of the Trinity in my life. Amen.

THE TRUTH:
The God Who Came Down

*T*HERE IS SOMETHING inexplicably wonderful about the way that God wanted to become intimately involved with people. The indwelling reality of the Holy Spirit is a truth that is sufficient to blow my mind.

Now all kinds of folk religions are full of stories about an arbitrary, capricious, transcendent being. They picture a god (or gods) who becomes momentarily involved in the real world only to withdraw swiftly in disgust. But the Christian gospel (the good news) is so very different.

No Christian can conceive of God only as the one who demands belief and faith, while hiding in a corner of the universe, determined to remain unknown and unknowable. The wonder of the Christian gospel is that there is one God, the Creator and ruler of heaven and earth, and He has no intention of keeping His distance!

- That is why God walked and talked with Adam in the Garden of Eden (Gen. 3:8–9).

- That is why God took Israel to be His people in a specially agreed relationship (Deut. 4:32–35).

- That is why God spoke to His people through prophets and continued to send prophets even though they were rejected one after another (Jer. 1:4–9).

- That is why God sent John the Baptist to prepare His people for the imminent birth on Planet Earth of His only begotten Son, Jesus Christ (John 1:7).

- That is why Jesus came, for supremely He brought His Father's love, fulfilled His mission by dying on a cross, and then at just the right time and in just the right place, broke the power of sin and death (Gal. 4:4).

This Jesus was totally different from any who had come before. He portrayed the love of His Father in a radical and unusual light. He ate, drank, spoke, was hungry, was thirsty, ran out of money, became tired,

9

and finally died at the hands of occupying forces obeying the wishes of His own people.

But this was not to be the end of the story. Jesus never came to Planet Earth in order to announce God's instructions for humankind; instead, He came to be the truth of God and to walk and talk with His people. If this God had just shouted out salvation from heaven, then we would have had to be satisfied with only hearing about it on earth. Instead, salvation came in the person and personality of Jesus. So God never shouted His message of salvation from out in the nether regions of space and then sent it to earth by remote control. Instead, the Truth of God came down here *to live among us.*

Although He ultimately returned from where He came, Jesus left His Holy Spirit to live and reign in His people. But the Holy Spirit was also sent with another function. He came as our Teacher to instruct us so that, after Jesus' departure, we would continue to learn about the Father and the Son (John 14:26).

He came so that we would understand the truth and be enabled to live in the light of what we had then learned.

THE GOD WHO IS HERE

The problem really boils down to the fact that while Christians generally find it easier to understand and relate to God the Father and God the Son, it is much harder to grasp hold of the concept of God the Holy Spirit.

We seem to find it relatively easy to wrap our minds around "a Father who creates" or "a Son who walks in history," but the notion of an apparently indefinable force that comes from God to live within His people is another matter entirely. Yet, the Holy Spirit is actually the Person of the Godhead who takes up residence within our lives. He cannot be separated from the Father and the Son, so He brings them along, too!

It seems to have become relatively so much easier to register the notion of a God who exists "out there" than to accept the idea of a living God who is right here in our lives, through His Holy Spirit who actually "indwells" us! It is this amazing reality that made the apostle Paul gasp in astonishment at the wonder of "the glorious riches of this mystery, which is Christ in you, the hope of glory" (Col. 1:27).

How can we, as mortal human beings, ever know the truth? The answer comes in two parts. First, our faith is not about an abstract and complex set of beliefs. It is about someone who, although God, came down to live and die for us. So spiritual truth is not just a discipline; it is a Person, and His name is Jesus. Second, the simple fact is that even then we may not understand. We need a Teacher, and who better than God Himself?

We can read our Bibles, but without the Spirit we will never be "guide[d] into all truth" (John 16:13). Sometimes the Holy Spirit whispers truths to us, and it is not until later that we recognize God's voice. It is not a matter of gaining human knowledge and expertise (although that can aid discussion), but it is more a matter of our allowing the Holy Spirit to reveal the depths of God to us. The miracle is that this is exactly what He has been sent to do.

THOUGHT FOR THE DAY

> For who among men knows the thoughts of a man except the man's spirit within him? In the same way no one knows the thoughts of God except the Spirit of God. We have not received the spirit of the world but the Spirit who is from God, that we may understand what God has freely given us.
>
> —1 CORINTHIANS 2:11–12

WAIT A MINUTE

Understanding spiritual truth can only happen by a work of the Spirit in your life. There is a twofold gain from receiving spiritual understanding. First, as we seek God and ask the Holy Spirit to deepen our understanding, we ultimately deepen our relationship with the Lord Jesus. Second, we will mature and become true guides to others in the things of God.

The key to gaining understanding is to get in tune with the Spirit. Then we will realize when God is revealing new things to us. This revelation may come through the Lord's Word, through somebody else, or perhaps through an audible voice. There are countless ways that the Spirit may wish to teach us about Jesus and the deep things of God, so we need to remain permanently tuned up and ready to go.

QUESTIONS TO CONTEMPLATE

1. Are you more dependent on human understanding or spiritual understanding?

2. Why?

SPACE TO REFLECT

Take time to spend with your Father, asking that His Spirit would fill you, teach you, and deepen your knowledge of Jesus.

A TIME TO PRAY

Please, Lord, will You reveal more spiritual truth to me? Help me to recognize Your voice speaking to me. I pray that I will no longer rely on my own human understanding but that Your Holy Spirit will guide me into a deeper understanding of You. Amen.

DAY 4

THE POWER
to Change the World

NOT ONLY DOES this Holy Spirit give us the power to live, but He also came to supply the power for us to serve. We were never intended to offer ourselves to God in our own strength. Instead, the Holy Spirit was sent to deliver what we would need and all that our human capabilities could never hope to provide.

That is why the Lord Jesus instructed the disciples to wait in Jerusalem for the Spirit to arrive upon them before they tried to go out and change the world for Him. Thank goodness He did! At the time, they were little more than a small band of 120 frightened, cowed, and defeated men and women. But in a matter of moments, the Holy Spirit had poured into them a spiritual power and energy that turned them into those who would go and turn their world upside down.

We are certainly entitled to ask what it was that changed their fear into faith. Why was this unpromising bunch suddenly transformed into world-beaters? The simple fact is this: if somehow the instructions of Jesus had persuaded them to venture out on this mission before the power of the Spirit arrived at Pentecost, then it could have produced little more than an overwhelming spiritual disaster.

So first they had to wait to receive power from God so that the work of God was done in His strength instead of being attempted through the feeble efforts of man.

One of the leading prophetic voices of the twentieth century was Dr. A. W. Tozer, a Christian and Missionary Alliance pastor. He once observed in his book *Paths to Power* that, "The church began in power, moved in power, and moved just as long as she had power. When she no longer had power, she dug in for safety and sought to conserve her gains."[1]

In our own daily lives we must avoid the danger of falling into the same trap. There is nothing that Satan would like more than to see us pushing the power of the Holy Spirit to one side and devoting our own strength and abilities to God's service. It is very natural to fall into that temptation, but it should be avoided at all costs.

The devil is not scared of us, but he is certainly fearful of the consequences that the power of the living God has within us.

MISSING PIECES, MISSING PERSON

Most of us would hate to admit it, but Christianity may have proved to be a little disappointing. The initial moment of surrender to the claims of Jesus on our lives was utterly genuine, but we missed out on the radical transformation that should have followed hard on the heels of our decision. In this way we have often struggled to live up to our promises.

Since then we have found that knowing about God has not proved adequate to enable us to live up to His standards. Our Christian lives have resembled the two-thousand-piece jigsaw puzzle that we once started to put together, only to discover that half the pieces were missing! That is exactly what life would be like if we were condemned to live without the Holy Spirit. But the great and gloriously liberating truth is that God never intended for us to live without His Spirit. Instead, He has provided His Holy Spirit to introduce us to His power that we might live in a whole new dimension.

Many of us know this to be the truth because that is exactly what has happened in our own lives. But if we try to pretend that everything has been OK from the start, then we are guilty of putting our heads in the sand. Trying to live in obedience to God while failing to draw power from the divine resources that He gave us is, quite frankly, stupid.

When we fall into the trap of trying to do our best for God through our own human energies instead of simply allowing Him to live through us, we inevitably set ourselves up for disaster. In fact, we can wake up one day to find that we may have been condemned to dwell in the relative shallows of our spiritual experience when God had originally called us to go deeper with Him.

The plain and simple fact is that when it comes to living for God, we just cannot do it alone! However, we do all have to admit that Scripture is quite clear that there is a Holy Spirit and that we are supposed to live in His fullness. The problem for most of us is getting to that point.

That is the reason why we are taking these fifty days and devoting them to God and to His divine will for our lives. It is no coincidence that this happens to be the same period from the glory of an empty tomb to the moment the Holy Spirit descended upon the disciples. They required the power of the Spirit in order to serve the living God, and so do we. It is time for all who long to serve Him in the way He intended to wait on Him for a deeper endowment of His power into our lives.

THOUGHT FOR THE DAY

Even on my servants, both men and women, I will pour out my
Spirit in those days, and they will prophesy.

—ACTS 2:18

WAIT A MINUTE

When Jesus sent the Spirit of God to His people, He did not leave out any
of the believers. His intention was for the Spirit to give every one of us the
power to serve Him. Why then do some of us still serve as though Pentecost never happened? Many of us today seem to find ourselves caught
in that period of fear and confusion after Christ rose from the dead. We
walk around as the disciples did: believing wholeheartedly in the Lord,
but not fully grasping the mission to which we are called.

Our call is to step out of that gap and to live in light of the message of
Acts. We should not continue striving in our own strength, but receive
the power of the Holy Spirit to serve Jesus so that we may fully understand who we are and what we are called for. Our Lord does not want us
to sit in the gap wondering why there seems to be so little change in our
lives; rather, He desires to radically transform us and equip us to be the
very hands and feet of Jesus.

QUESTIONS TO CONTEMPLATE

1. Have you accepted Christ as Lord but not experienced
   change?

2. What does the Lord want you to do?

SPACE TO REFLECT

The Lord Jesus may be asking you to step out in faith and to realize afresh
the power of His Spirit at work in your life.

A TIME TO PRAY

*Lord Jesus, I want to know more of Your power at work in my
life. I do not want to look at my life disappointed by the lack of
change. I want to know Your Spirit's power at work transforming me and helping me to change the world around me. Amen.*

THE LOVE:
GETTING RID OF THE FEAR

BANG...clunk...crash. The tortured gears of the ancient articulated truck echo through the Victorian manse, and six-year-old Ruth is jerked out of a deep sleep into what is rapidly becoming a familiar state of panic. She is sure that the Lord Jesus must be coming back, so once again she runs to her parents' room to see if they have been taken and she has been left behind.

Ruth grew to become a lovely lady and my wife. Like me, she is English. Originally born in Windsor, in the shadow of the queen's castle, Ruth came from a very strong Christian background. Her parents moved to a small village in the countryside, southeast of London. Her parents were the pastors of an Evangelical Free Church, which was relatively large for such a small village.

Their house was situated on the edge of a steep hill. Every night large trans-European container trucks took shortcuts through the village from the main road. When these massive vehicles arrived at the top of the hill, their engines would roar as they went through a manual gear change, and bright headlights would blaze through the thin curtains of the young girl's bedroom. Startled, Ruth would wake with that awful premonition that the Lord Jesus had returned, and she had been missed.

That is why she would find herself, feeling uncertain and apprehensive, making her sleepy way into her parents' bedroom, just to make certain that they were still there. When she discovered that they were still there, to her great relief, she would mumble prayers of commitment to affirm that she really did accept Jesus and wanted to be in heaven one day with her family.

Ruth would later discover the glorious liberating truth that spiritual answers are not found in fear but in faith. She discovered that the Lord Jesus wants to take us out of the darkness that provides a fertile soil for fear and into the light of His love. He brings us into a release from those unnatural bondages that we inflict upon ourselves and introduces us to a freedom that is allied to His truth.

The end result is even more exciting. If we will only surrender to Him the permission to do it, then He will simply take away all of our fears. Time and again, He will enter into our situation and whisper the words, "Don't be afraid" (Matt. 17:7).

ARE YOU AFRAID OF THE SPIRIT?

It is natural to be afraid of the dark. Most of us can readily sympathize with Ruth. Few of us could ever claim to live totally free of irrational fears! We sit glued to the TV screen watching programs like *Fear Factor* and grimace at the thought of having to do one of those stunts. All of us are familiar with our dislikes, which easily become our personal phobias. My phobia is snakes! It is easy to understand how confusion is born when we are not quite sure of who we are or where we are going.

It is uncertainty about the unknown that holds so many of us in its grip. When we are faced with the reality of a situation, we can rise up to face it, but contemplating it from a distance, now that is another matter indeed. It is the same for so many of us when it comes to the issue of life in the Holy Spirit. Too often we can be gripped by the fear of someone who is quite simply above and beyond our understanding.

Simply put, the Holy Spirit is supernatural. He extends beyond our human imagination, and so we can easily be frightened at the mere idea of what He might choose to do within our lives. Alternatively, we can become so overexcited at the thought of what dramatic experience or intervention the power of God will come up with next that we lose our concentration upon living for Him each day at a time. In other words, we are so anxious to progress from one spiritual high to the next that we forget to get on with the daily norm of loving and serving Jesus.

There can often be good reason for our eagerness or our discomfort. Often a past encounter has created this kind of imbalance. One friend may speak of the deep impression that was made on him when he watched someone being prayed for and, literally, saw the person's leg grow. Maybe another friend who was hungry for more of the Spirit in her life sought to speak in tongues, but at the meeting of a "charismatic" teacher found that things did not go as planned. Consequently, she was instructed to try to practice saying the alphabet backwards!

No wonder some are fascinated and still others are repelled whenever we speak of the Holy Spirit. The tragic result has been that the mere mention of His name has been enough to provoke some of us to overzealousness and others into unnatural resistance.

PERFECT LOVE
CASTS OUT ALL FEAR

So God gives us His Spirit in order that we might be supernaturally equipped to live as God Himself intended that we should. Although at first this may sound a little scary, we are talking about our Father! It is that same God of love who has brought us forgiveness and hope who now gives us His power to enable us to achieve all that He intended and become all that He wanted us to be.

Now His power is awesome. And it is right, in one way, that we should fear Him. We should honor, respect, and acknowledge His authority over our lives. But we need to be careful when our fear extends to the Holy Spirit and in a wrong way! For if we have surrendered our lives to the Lord Jesus, then His Spirit already inhabits us, and we do not have to be frightened of Him.

In fact, being filled with His perfect love, we can know freedom and deliverance from our natural fears. If we read the Bible from cover to cover, then we will discover that on no less than 366 occasions God instructs us not to be worried, anxious, or afraid. Those three sweet words "Do not fear," along with parallel words, are given so that we have one reference for every day of the year—and an extra one for leap years, too!

So often our suspicious nature, our paranoia, and our fear have crept into such a point that we have prevented the power of the Spirit from impacting our lives dramatically. The moment has come to abandon our fears and walk into the sunshine of all that the King has planned for us and all that His grace and love will bring us to enjoy!

THOUGHT FOR THE DAY

> For God did not give us a spirit of timidity, but a spirit of power, of love and of self-discipline.
>
> —2 TIMOTHY 1:7

WAIT A MINUTE

We can all ask the question as to why it is that we so often turn to our own resources and structures to manage and contain our lives. Often it is simply because we want to remain in control. But if we are to set the world on fire for Christ, we first need the fire of God to fill us and to release us into all that the King of kings has planned for us and that we cannot control!

So why not face up to the moment of truth? Let us put our fears to one side and start now. Let us begin to fearlessly tread where the disciples trod and prepare to move on in the power of the Spirit in all kinds of new and fresh ways.

The plain and simple truth is that the Spirit of God is not going to destroy us; instead, He has come to enable us to do great things. Perhaps all of us have to face moments in time when we need to discard our fears and welcome Him afresh into our lives.

QUESTION TO CONTEMPLATE

1. Why is it that people are afraid of the Holy Spirit who was sent from God and is God?

SPACE TO REFLECT

Realize that with God in control, there is nothing to fear. His Spirit's power will equip and enable you to change your nation for Him.

A TIME TO PRAY

Lord, forgive me for not allowing the Holy Spirit to move in power both in and through my life. Please take away my fears, and give me the confidence of knowing that Your love would never want to bring harm to my life. I pray that I might be open to all that You want to do in me and in the people that I meet. Lord, I don't want my life just to amount to my own human efforts; I want to know Your power and what it means to walk in it. Amen.

THE KING:
CHRIST IN US, THE HOPE OF GLORY

FOR EVANGELICAL CHRISTIANS the message of the Christian faith is plain and direct, and it is revealed in the Bible. It can be briefly summarized in the truth that God came down to earth as a man, demonstrated what life could be, and died on a cross to forgive and recover a people for Himself.

Despite constant rejections throughout history, the living God has continued to stretch out His hands of love toward His people throughout the length and breadth of His world. As the Creator He loved enough to allow His Son, Jesus, to die. Breaking out of the grave, Jesus now reigns at His Father's right hand in the glory of heaven. All plans and preparations approach completion for God's final act in history—taking His own people to be with Him forever.

There is, however, one fundamental problem. Humankind has never voluntarily fallen in with God's plans. He wants nothing but the best for us. Yet, consistently, we have rejected God's will and purposes.

But God does not just make demands on us. Instead He opens up to us His offer of a different kind of life from a cross, and then He extends to us the means by which we can live in that way. The good news is that this is no mere program to fulfill, but a person to live in and through us.

God would never merely push and impose His will upon our lives. Instead He provides for us the only means by which we can fulfill His purpose for our lives. He actually offers to give to us the power from Himself by His Holy Spirit. Through Him alone we are enabled to live in God's world and in God's way.

Only two questions remain. First, are we prepared to avail ourselves of His wonderful offer to us? Second, what kind of God is this who will actually provide the answer sheet for those who face His own test?

THREE IN ONE?

God wants each one who has committed his or her life to Jesus and received His forgiveness to spend eternity with Him. But what is He really like, this God with whom we will spend eternity? This question is a puzzling one because we are told that God is three Persons, but He is one God. How can this be? We need to freely acknowledge that we have more questions than answers!

This area of inquiry has been baffling church leaders for centuries, and it is important for us here. If the Holy Spirit is not a part of the God-head, then He is less than God and cannot achieve all in our lives that we would claim. The final judgment of the Christian faith is that one of the things that makes it unique is that it does not offer three gods but a Godhead of three distinct but indivisible Persons.

So this Godhead does not just consist of the Father and the Son, but it is a Trinity of Father, Son, and Holy Spirit. The Holy Spirit is sent from within the Godhead as a divine gift to all who respond to the love of Jesus and own Him as their Lord and King. He is, therefore, never less than God, but wherever He comes, the Father and the Son are present, too.

He is given in order that we might keep growing in our Christian lives. His supreme purpose is to bear witness to Jesus and to prepare us for eternal life. He brings the life and power of Jesus into our lives in order that we too might become more like Jesus. Put simply, the Spirit-filled life of Jesus becomes ours, so He is the one who is at work within us, getting us ready for an eternity of relationship with Him.

This is God's gift of love in that He recognizes the fact that we cannot make it in our Christian lives without Him. So instead of giving us some vague "force," He equips us by His very own Spirit. But because the Holy Spirit is one with God the Father and God the Son, we need to come to a greater understanding of how this relationship within the Trinity works out. We will never comprehend it fully because our minds are only human; we can never expect to fully understand the divine. Our finite minds were never intended to understand the infinite (God). If we could, then our God would have been reduced to human dimensions. He would be far too small.

Although God the Father took the initiative in creation, God the Son similarly leads in drawing us to God, and as the Holy Spirit inhabits our lives, we cannot make a total distinction. The Father does not create alone; the Son and Spirit are involved, too. Nor does the Son or Spirit act alone; they are intimately bonded together in an eternal union. So when the Holy Spirit comes into our lives, He does not enter alone; He always brings the Father and the Son with Him.

When we pray, it is to the Father, through the Son, but in the Holy Spirit. To emphasize this threefold character of God, Paul made this simple request for the church at Corinth. He asked that "the grace of the Lord Jesus Christ, and the love of God, and the fellowship of the Holy Spirit be with you all" (2 Cor. 13:14).

THOUGHT FOR THE DAY

All that belongs to the Father is mine. That is why I said the Spirit will take from what is mine and make it known to you.

—JOHN 16:15

WAIT A MINUTE

Not even the disciples who were present with Jesus before He was arrested completely understood who He was and what His mission on earth was really about. (See John 16:17ff.) Jesus tried to explain to His followers the relationship He had with the Father and the Holy Spirit, but perhaps to no avail!

This gives us comfort when we are still here today trying to understand the Three in One and that They are distinct but indivisible—if you know what that means! The best thing is for us not to strive to understand the Godhead, because we never will in its entirety—the reason being that we are not God! However, because we are called "sons of God," the Lord has put the Spirit's seal on our lives in order to help us to understand the truth about God (John 16:13). Amazingly, a lot of what we desire to know about our Lord and who He is can, and will, be revealed by the Spirit to us if we ask Him.

QUESTIONS TO CONTEMPLATE

1. Do you have trouble understanding who our Lord truly is?

2. Have you asked the Holy Spirit to reveal more truth to you? This will deepen your grasp on Him.

SPACE TO REFLECT

Be careful not to put God in a box, trying to pinpoint who He is. Remember that He is God, and therefore we will never correctly and completely conclude our thoughts this side of heaven.

A TIME TO PRAY

Lord, please help me to have a better grasp of who You really are so that I can pray effectively, serve powerfully, love completely, and lead people to a better understanding of my God. Amen.

THE SPIRIT:
WITHOUT HIM, WE WOULD BE NOWHERE

IT IS TRAGIC that for so long Christians have dismissed the Holy Spirit to the fringes of their spiritual interest when there is so much that He has done for us and wants to do within us. Little wonder that Satan has put so much effort into surrounding our understanding of the Holy Spirit with division and confusion. Somehow he does not mind us having head knowledge about Jesus so long as he can prevent us from enjoying the life of Jesus revealed by the Holy Spirit within us. Satan would love for us to be devoid of the power of the Spirit!

Paul, James, Peter, and John all write in every epistle (except in the two brief chapters of 2 and 3 John) about the Holy Spirit. They write of the fruit of the Spirit, the gifts of the Spirit, His guarding, resurrecting, witnessing, outpouring of love, renewing, interceding, demonstrating, gift impartation, life giving, transforming, sealing, promising, sanctifying, prophesying, and Scripture inspiring.

How could we leave Him out of our church life and teaching and, in some cases, from many areas of our lives? The problem is that far too many of us have become suspicious of the Spirit. So we have relegated the Holy Spirit to the edges of our belief and the circumference of our lives. How tragic that we, the Christian church, have been so creative in devising ways of managing without the Holy Spirit. We have replaced Him in so many areas of our lives with human resources and expertise. Instead of filling up at the gas pump, we have concentrated on attempting to invent our own substandard bootleg fuel! Struggling to find means of coping alone, we have totally ignored God's magnificent provision for us.

WITHOUT THE SPIRIT

To return to the crunch question: today, if we were without the Spirit, just where would we be? If the Spirit did not supernaturally equip us, then what would life be like?

1. There would be **no witness**—because without the Spirit, we would be left with only our own human resources for

serving Jesus and for sharing His love with others (Acts 1:8).

2.   There would be **no understanding**—the Holy Spirit wants to share with us all that we need to know because He is uniquely qualified to do so (1 Cor. 2:11).

3.   There would be **no worship**—without the Spirit our worship would be little more than mere routine expression to God (John 4:24).

4.   There would be **no gifts**—because without the Spirit we cannot be properly equipped for His service (1 Cor. 2:14, RSV).

5.   There would be **no power**—the Holy Spirit introduces a totally different dimension, a source of power for living, which emanates from God Himself in order to make us into radically different people (2 Tim. 1:7).

6.   There would be **no guidance**—devoid of a real revelation of all that God has prepared for us, we would be stuck in the confines of our own ambitions without the Spirit (Acts 16:7).

7.   There would be **no security**—the Holy Spirit is God's guarantee to us that God can take care of us now and in the future (1 John 3:24).

8.   There would be **no evidence**—without the Spirit we would have no signs and wonders as a vivid demonstration of God's reality and power (Acts 6:6, 8).

9.   There would be **no life**—the Spirit brings a quality of lifestyle that is unparalleled! (Rom. 8:6).

10.   There would be **no future**—we have something to look forward to because we know that God has deposited the Holy Spirit within us as a guarantee of what is to come (2 Cor. 1:22).

11.   There would be **no uniqueness**—there are so many religions and faiths that claim to bring information about God and man, past and future. For Christians, the Holy Spirit makes the difference.

12. There would be **no obedience**—now this is something that only God can bring. As we live in obedience to His direction we discover, not an easy route, but a God who never leaves us! (Acts 20:22–24).

13. There would be **no resurrection**—without the Holy Spirit, Jesus would still be dead, and so would we! (Rom. 8:11).

That great twentieth-century Puritan preacher Dr. Martyn Lloyd-Jones, who dominated the pulpit at London's Westminster Chapel for more than thirty years, once asked his parishioners if they were spiritually self-satisfied and complacent or if they were hungry for still more of God. So he asked in his rich vein of Welsh eloquence, "Got it all? Well, if you have 'got it all,' I simply ask, in the name of God, why are you as you are? If you have got it all, why are you so unlike the New Testament Christians? Got it all? Got it all at your conversion? Well, where is it, I ask?"

Without the Holy Spirit we will never learn what it truly means to live in God's world God's way! Nor will that life ever be adequately demonstrated before a watching world. The Holy Spirit is not to be treated with disregard, but with love, respect, and gratitude. So we need not adopt an attitude of either fear or indifference toward Him, but instead we should develop a hunger for the only one who can form the life of God within us.

THOUGHT FOR THE DAY

I will give you a new heart and put a new spirit in you; I will remove from you your heart of stone and give you a heart of flesh. And I will put my Spirit in you...

—EZEKIEL 36:26–27

WAIT A MINUTE

When we actually begin to break it down and really come to grips with who and what the Holy Spirit does and is, our minds are completely blown away! Surely when we get our minds around the character and nature of the Spirit of God, the question that we undoubtedly find ourselves asking is, "How can we possibly leave Him out?" Life with Him is real and fulfilling; without Him we are left with worldly hearts of stone.

Consider all the aspects of how the Holy Spirit opens our eyes, hearts, and minds in a new way. For so long our focus has been on the Father or on the Son, yet the Lord is not complete without the Third Person—the Holy Spirit. With all the attributes laid out for us in Scripture and high-lighted in today's reading, we do not need to be suspicious anymore. We can turn from depending on our own human resources and expertise because we serve a Lord who can give us so much more.

QUESTIONS TO CONTEMPLATE

1. Have you been managing your own life, relying on your own skills to cope?

2. In what ways?

3. What would your life look like with/without the Spirit?

SPACE TO REFLECT

Take a couple of the attributes of the Spirit from today's reading from anywhere you choose. For example: His guarding and His sealing. Allow who He really is to take root in your heart and life.

A TIME TO PRAY

Lord, thank You that You have such a diverse character and nature. Lord, help me not to depend on my own resources or manage my own life. Father, I pray that as I begin to understand who Your Spirit truly is, You will transform me into a person dependant upon You working in and through me. Amen.

WEEK TWO

THE HOLY SPIRIT: GOD'S MAP BOOK

Jesus refers to the Spirit as the *Paraclete*, meaning to "call alongside." He comes alongside to help us, to speak for us, to comfort, encourage and advise us.

—COLIN DYE
LIVING IN THE PRESENCE

Jesus doesn't promise that the Holy Spirit will *control* us. He doesn't promise that He will *drive* us. He doesn't say that the Holy Spirit will *force* us to do anything. He says He will *guide* us.

—CHARLES STANLEY
THE WONDERFUL SPIRIT-FILLED LIFE

How to know the will of God can be one of the greatest challenges of the Christian life, and often one of the greatest frustrations of the young Christian life.

—MAX ANDERS
*JUST THE FAQ*s ABOUT THE HOLY SPIRIT*

THE GUIDE:
GOD'S GLOBAL POSITIONING SYSTEM

I REMEMBER WHEN my oldest son, Kris, was only six years of age. Whenever I came home after having been away for a few days, I found that I could suggest just about any activity to him and he would demonstrate an unusual degree of compliance. So we would take the dog for a walk, play soccer together, or go shopping in town. Any suggestion would receive the one-word reply: "Great!" He was so pleased to have his daddy home that he was happy with pretty much any suggestion that I made. He just wanted to be with his dad.

Later in life, when teenage years arrived, things did indeed begin to change. He became even more aware of the fact that he possessed a will of his own! He would express his own desires, and if they conflicted with mine, then a meaningful dialogue would arise! If disagreement continued, then I faced a serious choice. Either I had to attempt to impose my will, or leave it up to my son and trust that either he or I would learn lessons from our mistakes. Much would always depend on just how serious we each felt that the issue really was.

However, because I am not God, the analogy naturally breaks down. Kris's course of action may actually prove to be better than mine. With a loving God who is totally committed to us, that possibility cannot exist. He loves us so much that He can only desire the best for His people.

THE GOD WHO WANTS US TO HEAR

Sometimes Christians become very worried about guidance. They wonder if they have missed out somewhere. God does not want that. It is right for us to look for God's way, but not to be worried and concerned. God wants us to experience joy in finding His way, and we are more likely to do that if we get on with living where we are and working on our relationship with Jesus. Then we will be ready to hear God's voice when He wants us to move. If we start worrying about the next step too soon, we'll start imagining all sorts of things that aren't really there. "Seek first his kingdom and his righteousness, and all these things will be given to you as well. Therefore do not worry about tomorrow" (Matt. 6:33–34).

It is all too easy to become over concerned with the detail of God's plan for our lives and lose sight of His overall purpose. The wonderful truth is that God's main purpose for us is to make us like Jesus. "Those whom God had already chosen he also set apart to become like his Son" (Rom. 8:29, GNT).

God never wants us to miss His way for us.

Paul and his companions discovered this when they wanted to go to Bithynia against the will of God, because "the Spirit of Jesus would not allow them to" (Acts 16:7). This is more than just an indication of His loving commitment to us. He longs that we will not go astray. However well intentioned we may be, our mistaken notions of what would be right for us may often mean that the Holy Spirit has to take action in order to prevent us from wandering off in the wrong direction.

So He does not barge into our lives and impose His will and purpose upon us. Instead He has sent His own Holy Spirit into our lives to be our guide and our mentor. The Holy Spirit leads us into God's best way for our lives and enables us to fulfill our God-given destiny.

But God does still leave it in our hands to demonstrate through our obedience the right and necessary response to the guide He has provided for us. His guidance remains optional, because He has not chosen to make us a part of some rigid, automatic process. He has never been content to just wind us up as some mere clockwork robot, preprogrammed to conform to His will for our lives. Basically, He waits to know whether we wish to listen to the voice of His Spirit as He seeks to offer direction for our lives or if we are stubbornly determined to stick with the folly of only wanting to persist with following our own inclinations.

So He does not push His guidance on us. The living God is no arbitrary deity just trying to get His own way, but He longs to bring fulfillment to our lives. He looks for a people who will trust Him as their Creator to bring the best for them, a people whom He can involve in the unfolding of His purposes in their nation and His world. That is why He does not leave us to blindly pursue our own pathway; He offers the highest quality of guide that this world has ever known.

Thought for the Day

When they [Paul and his companions] came to the border of Mysia, they tried to enter Bithynia, but the Spirit of Jesus would not allow them to.

—Acts 16:7

Wait a Minute

Paul and his companions were filled with the Spirit of God; therefore, they intuitively knew that they were not to enter Bithynia. Wow! What an amazing testimony to the powerful guidance of God in the lives of mere men!

Surely we can expect the Holy Spirit to guide us in the same way. So why then do we hold on to our own decisions, somehow strangely confident that they will be better choices? This is not a clever decision when we consider what wonderful guidance could be bestowed upon us. But that can only apply if we were to allow the Spirit to lead us into all the fullness of guidance, direction, and empowerment that God has intended for every one of us.

This guidance comes from *knowing* Jesus. Paul was familiar with the Lord's guidance because he *knew* Him. First, we must be willing to surrender our lives to Him and let Him lead, which requires trust and dependency. Second, we need to get to know Him intimately to be able to recognize and know His guiding lights.

Questions to Contemplate

1. What aspects of life do you find hard to surrender to Him? For example, how do you arrive at choices of where to live, where to work, or whom to marry?

2. Are these things that you choose and then ask God to bless your decisions? Or are you prepared to allow the Spirit of God to guide you throughout the course of your life?

3. Have you already made a conscious decision to surrender to His direction?

SPACE TO REFLECT

How much more should you actively surrender your agenda to the Lord?
What changes could you make to your lifestyle in order to allow the Spirit to guide you precisely to where He wants you to go?

A TIME TO PRAY

Lord, I surrender to You the direction and decisions for my life. Will You please lead me and then bless me? Lord, teach me to live in far greater dependence upon You so that I may rely completely on the guidance of Your Holy Spirit and clearly determine His leading on my life today, this week, and in the months and years to come. Amen.

DAY 9

THE DIRECTOR:
WE ARE UNDER INSTRUCTIONS

AUTHOR DENYS PARSONS relates the following story in the book *The Best of Shrdlu*:

> A baby rabbit fell into a quarry's mixing machine yesterday and came out in the middle of a concrete block. But the rabbit still had the strength to dig its way free before the block set.
>
> The tiny creature was scooped up with thirty tons of sand, then swirled and pounded through the complete mixing process....With the thirty tons of sand, it was dropped into a weighing hopper and carried by conveyor to an overhead mixer where it was whirled around with gallons of water.
>
> From there the rabbit was swept to a machine, which hammers wet concrete into blocks, by pressure of one hundred lbs. per square inch. The rabbit was encased in a block eighteen inches long, nine inches high and six inches thick. Finally the blocks were ejected on to the floor to dry and the dazed rabbit clawed itself free! We cleaned him up, dried him by the electric fire, then he hopped away!

Many have seen their own lives reflected in just this kind of picture: a poor innocent caught in the vast machine of life, only just managing to escape, driven helplessly along by whatever the vicissitudes of life choose to throw at us.

For the Christian, such a picture completely fails to capture the truth. In giving our lives to Jesus Christ, we have placed ourselves under His control. So why, then, do so many accidents of life occur, especially those that clearly, to our minds, could not be in the will and purpose of God?

The answer lies clearly within the kind of redirection that the living God longs to provide for us. God employs unusual and mysterious courses of action to fulfill His divine purposes in us. After all, if He were content to work within our own finite categories of action and direction, then He would be less than who He is. It is precisely because He is God that He operates in ways where we have to catch up with Him. So it is never sufficient for us to merely expect Him to be content to bless whatever agenda we lay before Him for our lives. As a loving Father who

35

knows what is best for His children, He always wants us to be obedient to Him as He acts within His own will.

So no Christian can ever be regarded as being merely at the mercy of a vicious, fallen world. We are far from being only helpless victims. Unlike the rabbit, we have been provided with the One who is the finest guide through life—the Holy Spirit—God Himself.

Parting Gift

Those who worship within a Catholic church setting are familiar with the need for a spiritual counselor or director in certain situations, and that is exactly what Pentecost delivered—the Holy Spirit—my personal guide.

Before Jesus died, He made what some have seen as His "last will and testament." He bequeathed:

- His body to Joseph of Arimathea
- His clothes to the soldiers who were killing Him
- His mother to His beloved disciple, John
- His spirit to His Father

But He left to His disciples a very special promise in these words: "Peace is what I leave with you; it is my own peace that I give you" (John 14:27, GNT). He appointed no executor to ensure that the provisions of His will were fulfilled. Instead, it was after His resurrection that He personally visited them in order to ensure that they received His parting gift. Without creating any damage, He broke through a wall in order to greet them with the words, "Peace be with you" (John 20:19).

The parting gift of Jesus to His followers was a peace that the world can never provide, a peace that only the Holy Spirit can give. Paul comments about this peace in his letter to the Colossians: "The peace that Christ gives is to guide you in the decisions you make" (Col. 3:15, GNT).

Jesus emphasized this same truth when He made this marvelous promise to His followers. He pledged that we would not be left as orphans in a pagan world. Instead, the Holy Spirit would come to us, and "he will lead you into all the truth" (John 16:13, GNT).

In other words, the Holy Spirit has come to direct our lives, and the peace of God rules in our hearts to confirm that guidance.

GOD IS AT WORK IN US!

In order to keep us traveling along His own straight and narrow pathway for our lives, God may fence us in—both in time and in place—to keep us in the center of His will. The Holy Spirit may sometimes create major obstacles to keep us from wandering away, but these are actions of love to prevent us from hurting ourselves too deeply or damaging our lives too much.

The Spirit of God is concerned about the direction of our lives. God uses the story of Hosea and his relationship with his unfaithful wife, Gomer, to illustrate how His people, Israel, have lived in relationship to the Lord.

> But I will fence her in with thornbushes. I will block the road to make her lose her way. When she runs after her lovers, she won't be able to catch up with them. She will search for them but not find them. Then she will think, "I might as well return to my husband because I was better off with him than I am now."
>
> —HOSEA 2:6–7, NLT

Still He leaves obedience as our response to His grace.

Even then, we are not left to cope alone. We may wonder how things happen. They happen because Jesus never stops working within our lives. Through His Holy Spirit, He is endeavoring to teach us the lessons of what it means to really live in God's world and how we can begin to live in it God's way.

That is why Jesus told His disciples they would be better off without Him! Impossible as it may be for us to believe that, He actually said that we are in a better position! "I am telling you the truth: it is better for you that I go away, because if I do not go, the Helper will not come to you" (John 16:7).

Now a human spiritual director can bring us helpful words of advice and guidance, but he or she cannot provide the resources for us to fulfill their proposals. The Holy Spirit is different. He does not just direct the traffic of our life circumstances from outside, but from within.

Because the Spirit has come to us, we do not have to be satisfied with God walking alongside. We can actually know Him living within us. He has come to bring both His direction and empowering to our lives!

THOUGHT FOR THE DAY

Therefore I will block her path with thornbushes; I will wall her in so that she cannot find her way. She will chase after her lovers but not catch them; she will look for them but not find them. Then she will say, "I will go back to my husband as at first, for then I was better off than now."

—HOSEA 2:6–7

WAIT A MINUTE

One of the problems with directors is that sometimes they may not agree with us! It is like that with the Holy Spirit; we will find out that there will be occasions when His ways are definitely not ours.

Often we can assume that we have heard what we are supposed to do, so we launch into it, neglecting to ask God when His timing was right. The Spirit of God does not want us to pin Him down and limit His ways. They are so much greater than our human understanding and cannot be caged. Look at Hosea's wife—the Spirit's ways were definitely not her ways! Now He doesn't deal with us severely unless it is required, but He can put us in a situation where we had no intention of going, at a time that we least expect, to suit His divine purposes.

Even then we can find great security and assurance in the fact that although we make all manner of mistakes trying to understand how the Holy Spirit is guiding us, thankfully, He is still gracious and works through us. Despite our errors, He is our Supreme Director.

QUESTIONS TO CONTEMPLATE

1. Do you ever try to box the Spirit's guidance, wrapping it up with a neat little bow?

2. Do you try to manipulate Him to agree with you? Why?

SPACE TO REFLECT

Ask the Lord to bring to mind how you went about making your last big or little decision. Did you allow the Spirit of God to reveal His plans? What process did you go through to determine His will? Was He responsible for the final direction?

A TIME TO PRAY

Lord, I want to consider Your timing as well as where and with whom You want me to go. Please prompt me by Your Spirit so that I know deep in my soul when You are trying to show me what to do. Amen.

THE LISTENERS:
LESSONS FOR LIFE

WE WANT TO know and do the will of God in our lives, we want to follow His direction, but that still leaves us with a problem. Too often we end up in the same position as the apostle Paul, who freely confessed that, "I have the desire to do what is good, but I cannot carry it out. For what I do is not the good I want to do; no, the evil I do not want to do—this I keep on doing" (Rom. 7:18–19). Doing the will of God represents a phenomenal challenge for us, but so does knowing what that will is in the first place.

So how, then, can we hear and understand what God wants us to do? It is so difficult to be sure when God is speaking to us. All too often we are left wondering if it was God speaking or if it was just our imagination. "How can I be sure that I've heard the Holy Spirit's voice?" If I had a dollar for every time I've been asked that question, I'd be a wealthy man! God's Spirit has so many ways of guiding us, some dramatic, some gentle, but very rarely anything as dramatic as writing on the wall.

How can we know God's way for our lives? What hints does He give us? There are certainly some key points to help us discern more of His will and ways for us.

1. Through circumstances
This is the most common manner through which Christians expect to receive their guidance, but we must be very careful to be certain that it is the Holy Spirit's hand guiding each situation. It is here that we need the peace of God to act as the signal to our hearts.

Several years ago Ruth and I found ourselves in a real dilemma while we were engaged in seeking direction for the future. I felt every circumstance in this particular situation was seemingly pointing forward, but Ruth felt a real absence of peace within her. We proceeded very slowly, believing that God would either clearly confirm this check or dismiss it. A few days later, the Lord brought His word to us through a close friend that we should not take another step. As a man, I might struggle to acknowledge that my wife was right, but I have observed over the years that the woman is often more sensitive and open to divine direction than the man.

2. By following

God's intention has never been just to prod us from behind. His call to disciples is always, "Follow Me." In other words, God's Spirit will always travel ahead of us, preparing the ground so that we can follow in *His* footsteps. If we choose not to follow, then we soon lose that sense of peace. Although we cannot just fall in and out of the Spirit of God, we can obey or disobey.

3. Through Scripture

God never changes His mind or contradicts His Word. As the psalmist said, "Your word is a lamp to my feet and a light for my path" (Ps. 119:105). Any claim to guidance that goes against the clear teachings of the Bible must be immediately rejected. Following Jesus must always involve obedience to the Spirit's Word in Scripture. Paul made this plain when he said, "The Holy Spirit was right when he said to our ancestors through Isaiah the prophet..." (Acts 28:25, NLT).

4. Through people

We must proceed with caution. God's Spirit can lead us through other people, but only within the confines of His revealed Word in Scripture. Paul knew how to reject advice as well as receive it. "By the power of the Spirit they told Paul not to go to Jerusalem. But when our time with them was over, we left and went on our way" (Acts 21:4–5, GNT). However well intentioned the advice, we must assess it and test its value before the Lord. Often when God intends something for us, He will reveal it to more than one person and confirm it for us as well!

5. In dreams

God does not try to hide His will from us. Sometimes He intervenes while we are asleep. Paul experienced this: "That night Paul had a vision in which he saw a Macedonian standing and begging him, 'Come over to Macedonia and help us!'" (Acts 16:9, GNT). Immediately he responded to God's call.

We need to be careful to judge our dreams and visions correctly. Sometimes they may be divinely or demonically inspired, although the latter is unusual for Christians. What is more likely is that it may be mere fantasy. We need to check carefully with the Lord, especially if we are not living in a close relationship with Him.

6. By listening

We hear from God in so many ways. He can speak through inspired speech, word of knowledge, word of wisdom, prophecy, or through a gentle nudge from the Spirit. (This will be experienced as a quiet inner conviction, but we must be careful; our own imagination may well mislead.) God can communicate through a sense of agreement with others.

LISTENING FOR BEGINNERS

Although there are a variety of ways in which God leads us, we recognize one common factor. His direction for our lives stems from a deep, personal relationship with Jesus through the Holy Spirit. It is only as we surrender our lives in an ever-deepening commitment to Jesus and listen for the voice of the Spirit that His purposes for us become clear.

Ultimately everything will emanate from, and will revolve around, our own intimacy with Jesus. If we love Him, we will listen to Him, and we will be familiar with His voice. This becomes the most important factor in our lives; it enables us to hear how the Spirit is directing our lives. The Lord does not want His people to strive for intimacy; He simply wants us to surrender our will to a life governed by the Spirit.

All of these practices will require a biblical undergirding and a confirmation of divine approval. The guarantee of revelation lies in the activity of the early church under the Spirit's direction, which was well illustrated at Antioch where they gathered to fast and pray. It was in that context "the Holy Spirit said to them" (Acts 13:2, GNT).

One reason that the Lord wants us to be intimate with Him is so that we will be aware when He is revealing His plans. We all need to remember that even when we believe that God has spoken, such revelation always needs to be tested. Always be cautious about declaring, "The Lord says." A more appropriate declaration is, "I believe the Lord is saying…" Too quickly we assume that God has said and done all that He wants to do. We even ignore the possibility that we may have been guilty of trying to get Him to divinely sanction what were only our human desires in the first place.

The real proof is often ultimately revealed by the wonderful way God works out His purposes for us. Circumstances are not often a good initial evidence of guidance, but they can often provide a great confirmation!

THOUGHT FOR THE DAY

I will instruct you and teach you in the way you should go; I will counsel you and watch over you. Do not be like the horse or mule, which have no understanding but must be controlled by bit and bridle or they will not come to you.

—PSALM 32:8–9

WAIT A MINUTE

The danger is to focus so much on how the Lord is guiding us that we become self-centered, ultimately diverting from God's overall purposes. The Lord does want us to hear from Him and respond, but His heart is also for us not to waste time. He wants to use us where we are right now. However, God mercifully does provide divine direction to His children through His Spirit. There are many ways that He speaks to us. We need to become used to hearing His voice or seeing His will revealed before our very eyes.

QUESTIONS TO CONTEMPLATE

1. How would you describe your relationship with the Lord?

2. Do you struggle to know how the Spirit is guiding you?

3. In what ways can you become more certain of what He is saying?

SPACE TO REFLECT

Allow the Lord to open up your mind to the ways that He wishes to speak to you today. Consider those ways in which He most often chooses to reveal His plans in your own situations.

A TIME TO PRAY

Almighty God, please increase my understanding of how You guide Your people. Forgive me for sometimes limiting Your right of direction on my life. As I seek to serve You, please help me to recognize Your voice and to act accordingly, and then please arrange Your own confirmation for me. In the name of Jesus, amen.

THE COUNSELOR:
THE ONLY INFALLIBLE GUIDE

WHEN ASKED WHO the Holy Spirit really is to us, most of us either give a blank look or we begin to recount what He means in our lives. However, individual experience may not always be the correct place to start.

When God intended to reveal His nature, will, and identity to humankind, He determined to do so supremely in His Son. When He wanted to place on record His activities with the inhabitants of this planet, He chose to do so in a book. So if we want to know what the Spirit of God is like and how He operates within the lives of God's people, then we need to turn to the pages of the Bible.

It has been pointed out—and rightly so—that too many Christians have failed to challenge that artificial Trinity of Father, Son, and Holy Scripture. Nothing could be further from the truth. While the Bible is the infallible word of God and is truly God-breathed, it also affirms the third member of the Trinity—the Holy Spirit.

Throughout the pages of the Bible it is always assumed that the Holy Spirit is no more and no less than God Himself. He is called "the Spirit of the Lord" (1 Kings 18:12), the gift of the Father (Luke 11:13), and "the Spirit of Jesus" (Acts 16:7). Paul clearly announces, "The Lord is the Spirit" (2 Cor. 3:17).

So when Peter rebukes Ananias for his attempted deception, he boldly announces, "You have lied to the Holy Spirit....You have not lied to men but to God" (Acts 5:3–4). And when Jesus spoke about the "unforgivable sin," He was speaking of rejecting, not the Father or even Jesus Himself, but the Holy Spirit (Matt. 12:30–32). We may mock or curse our fellow human beings, but blasphemy is a sin that can only be committed against God Himself.

It is because the Holy Spirit is God that Scripture describes Him as possessing all those essential hallmarks, which are the sole privilege of God Himself. So what is His character? He is:

☞ *Holy*—God cannot deny His own character, therefore, in the same way that God is completely pure and totally unblemished, so is the "Holy" Spirit! (1 Cor. 6:19).

☞ *Eternal*—If God were limited by time and space, then He could not be God. The Creator cannot be limited by His creation, nor could God die or face extinction.

☞ *Living*—There was never a moment when the Holy Spirit was not there, and there will never be a funeral service for Him, for He will always be there for us.

☞ *God*—If He is to be perfect and holy in His character, then He must be more than human. But to last beyond the vast aeons of time and be eternal, He has to be divine. So when Scripture says that the Holy Spirit is eternal (always was and always will be), then it is actually affirming that He must be God (Heb. 9:14).

The Holy Spirit is, therefore, no more or no less than the holy, eternal, living God.

WHO IS THIS HOLY SPIRIT?

We live in an age when many have become familiar with the words, "Come, Holy Spirit." Yet I wonder if we really are aware of what we are asking for! Too often we have been content to view the Holy Spirit as just a useful adjunct to our lives.

Yet, He must never be reduced to that level. For He came as God Himself to be the love of God on fire dwelling within us and the wisdom of God available to guide us into all truth (John 16:13). As such, He is the supreme Counselor available anywhere in this world today.

The term *counselor*, or helper, is a legal term, and it refers to any person who helps someone who is in trouble with the law. In the same way, the Holy Spirit will always be there to defend and stand by God's people, but in this case the range of the term is far broader than a mere "counsel for the defense." For the Spirit is also called the "Spirit of Truth," so He is uniquely qualified to make our defense. In the Spirit of Truth, we have a counselor who, by definition, cannot get it wrong!

In John's Gospel, the Holy Spirit is referred to in various translations as the "helper," "counselor," "comforter," and "advocate." In fact, He is a combination of all four: an advocate to plead our case; a counselor to guide; a comforter to console us in times of trouble; and a helper to assist us to do all those things that we can never do alone.

But the picture that the translators of the King James Version envisaged of the Comforter was not of a sympathetic ear! If we go back in history, then we get a clearer picture of what was actually meant by the word, and it is not a comfortable picture.

The Holy Spirit is the one who mobilizes us for battle. His anointing is for the healing of the brokenhearted, the defeat of the enemy, and the proclamation of the gospel to the poor. The apostle Paul assures us that the Spirit is the guarantee that we shall receive what God has promised his people" (Eph. 1:14).

So far from being content with being our divine counselor and guide who is available to point us in the right direction, this Holy Spirit is also the one who equips us in order that we may fulfill all that God wills for us. Not only does He lead us, but He enables us to arrive at our destination as well. How can He do this? The short answer is that He is God Himself, and therefore nothing is impossible for Him.

THOUGHT FOR THE DAY

Then the LORD said, "My Spirit will not contend with man forever, for he is mortal; his days will be a hundred and twenty years."
—GENESIS 6:3

WAIT A MINUTE

The more we read about the Holy Spirit and allow Him to change our lives, the more we understand about His character. What we then discover is the amazing fact that actually the Spirit of God possesses all the essential characteristics of God Himself. Undoubtedly and inevitably, because He is God! The Spirit is therefore:

- Holy—unblemished and pure (1 Cor. 6:19)
- Eternal—always was and always will be (Heb. 9:14)
- Omnipotent—all-powerful (Luke 1:35–37)
- Omnipresent—exists everywhere simultaneously (Ps. 139:7)
- Omniscient—knows everything (1 Cor. 2:10–11)

Wow! What a gift to us! Not only is He all these things, but He is also personal. This means that the extensive grace of God enables us to actually have a living relationship with Him. It is amazing to think again about some of the attributes of the Holy Spirit; it is so easy to forget just how powerful and vital He is to our lives. It is unbelievable that this God would dwell in us! And not just in spiritual superstars or those who seem purer believers than us, but this gift is given to every one of the people of God.

QUESTIONS TO CONTEMPLATE

1. If the Holy Spirit really is God and He dwells within you, what does that mean for your life?

2. How then should you live?

SPACE TO REFLECT

Consider the qualities of the Holy Spirit (listed above) and allow the truth of who He is to impact your life afresh today.

A TIME TO PRAY

Father, I am blown away by how awesome You are. Your Spirit's power and authority are too phenomenal for my human mind to grasp. I pray that You will help me to realize who You are and how that knowledge affects my life. Amen.

THE DETAILS:
GETTING IT RIGHT

THE HOLY SPIRIT is always at work to bring our lives into conformity with the will of God for us. He does this so that we may be able to actively cooperate with God's own purposes through our lives. In a very real sense, guidance comes from the Holy Spirit in order that we might fulfill the role of sometimes acting as literally the hands and feet of Jesus!

The Spirit of God is concerned about our lives. Although He has not programmed us to act like robots under His direct manual control, He does want us to involve Him in our decisions. Not only is He concerned with where we are going, but He is also concerned about who accompanies us on the journey and about when we go. God is also concerned about us having the wrong timing and the wrong direction.

Nor is it just the concept with which He is concerned, but the practice of getting there is equally significant to Him. Too often we have become complacent and considered that providing we use the right words and attempt to move toward the right objective, then that would be sufficient to please the Lord. But we have to go further than that, for God does not just want us to be aware of His plans and achievements; He intends us to fulfill them as well.

It has often been alleged that "the devil is in the details!" Now, I am not sure that I would want to concede that much ground to him, but it is certainly true that even when we know where we are going, it can be hard to get there! He will certainly do everything in his power to frustrate God's purposes, while the Holy Spirit is busily employed making sure that we are enabled and empowered to fulfill them.

ARRIVING AT OUR DESTINATION

Mozambique is situated on the southeast coastline of Africa. Looking at a map, you see it looks like a long, thin stretch of land extending for many hundreds of miles. On one particular occasion I was traveling south to north with some church leaders from the States on a light aircraft piloted by two smartly dressed South Africans. At first impression, they looked as if they knew where they were going, but then again, how wrong can you be?

We were looking for a small, remote town called Chicualacuala, and we soon realized that our pilots were lost. This was confirmed when one of them turned round and blithely asked, "Does anyone know where the airstrip is? Or how about the town?" After an initial muted panic, we all calmed down. Despite circling around the anticipated location, we found that we could identify neither the town nor the landing strip. So with fuel running low, we reluctantly turned back.

Our disappointment lay in the fact that Chicualacuala lay on the very edge of the famine-stricken area. We were aware that a large number of African pastors would have traveled long distances in their malnourished condition in order to meet with us. For some we knew had largely built their hopes upon our visit. In their churches, both adults and children alike were facing a bleak future without food. These pastors would have been only too aware that we might have meant the last opportunity for telling the world of the perilous position of their congregations.

Still, there was nothing we could do. At least we knew that the second part of our team would stay there with the vehicles awaiting our arrival—or so we thought. Then at 2:45 a.m. there came a hammering at our hotel door. My country director had bad news. After hours of attempting to raise the second team by radio he had finally succeeded. They had been watching with dismay as we circled Chicualacuala and saw when our plane flew away. So they too had given up and had made the eight-hour drive back to our base. We knew that if we continued in the morning, the pastors had all returned to their villages, and now the vehicles had gone, too.

Yet I knew in my heart that we were meant to go there. I have been wrong on many occasions, as my wife would tell you, but on this occasion I felt that the Holy Spirit forcefully impressed upon me how important it was for us to still make this trip. So despite the obvious reluctance and unvoiced fears of some of my colleagues, we duly set off the next day but this time we had a different set of navigational directions!

Once we landed we found that no less than half the town had turned out to greet us, and we discovered that the local government official actually did have a couple of vehicles (the only ones available in the area). So much for going unnoticed! The even better news was that he was quite prepared and willing to offer them to us for the day.

After dividing the team in two and setting off in different directions, we arrived in the village of Mapai a couple of hours later. The pastor of the Assemblies of God church was delighted to see us. He had been one of those who had made the long trek to Chicualacuala the day before and was overjoyed to now meet us. He guided us around the village so we could see the little church and meet some of those who were now too weak to walk. Their meager diet mainly consisted of dried worms and wild fruit. Then we came across a man the pastor did not know. We crouched on the ground alongside him and asked if he would tell us about himself, which he was happy to explain.

"I come from this village and left many years ago. I was a Christian then, but I went to Maputo (the capital city), and there I lost Jesus. Now I have finished with my life. So I came back to the village, and I am sitting beneath this tree and waiting to die. The reason that I am not dead yet is that the people in the hut next to me had enough rice left for one more meal. After they ate, there were still some grains of rice stuck to the side of the saucepan, and they gave them to me. Now I will die."

It was not difficult to discern the fact that this was a divine appointment. Had we arrived at our planned destination the day before we would only have met the pastors at a central destination. We would never have been in this village, and we would have missed meeting this man. Kneeling there in the dust and the dirt, the pastor and I had the joy of leading him back to Jesus.

But this was not the end of the story. One of the church leaders, a businessman, offered to pay for food supplies to be provided for this man, the church, and the local churches for the entire area. In fact, on my next trip to Mozambique, I was excited to witness two pastors setting out on the long drive to deliver the latest round of food supplies through the churches to these people in such desperate need.

I am constantly amazed at the way in which God organizes things, for the timing and location of our entire visit had been divinely engineered to meet the needs of that man and of the local community. It is a simple fact that the Lord will often take us to situations where we had no previous intention of going and at a time when we least expect! What is required of us is that we be willing to go there. However, it is so easy to do the opposite and to let our minds be controlled by the sinful nature.

There are two basic results. One is that we can wander into flagrant and deliberate sin. We can assume that no one knows what we are thinking or can see what we are doing, so we get up to all kinds of things that we know are wrong. The other is that we resist God's leading or allow ourselves to be diverted, so that we end up missing out on what He had planned for us, and that is sin as well!

In both cases we seem to constantly forget that the Lord does not miss anything. He shines a light in dark places to expose both our sins of commission (what we do intentionally and deliberately) and our sins of omission (what we simply fail to do).

On the other hand, if we choose to live in accordance with the Spirit of God and give Him control, He can extinguish the flaming arrows of the evil one and strengthen us to overcome battles mentally, physically, and emotionally. He will take us and lead us into all that God has for us, and He will guard us from everything that the enemy throws at us. All we need to do is to surrender to the Spirit's direction instead of the control of our own inherently sinful human nature.

THOUGHT FOR THE DAY

Those who live according to the sinful nature have their minds set on what that nature desires; but those who live in accordance with the Spirit have their minds set on what the Spirit desires.

—ROMANS 8:5

WAIT A MINUTE

We have a tendency to go about our lives our way, and then so often we get things wrong. It is sometimes very difficult to surrender control. Jesus admitted that He could do nothing by Himself (John 5:19, 30). He allowed the Father to lead Him. Why then do we not follow His lead? Why are we so stubborn?

If the Son of God paused to listen to His Father, why don't we? We are called to follow the example of Jesus: to wait, to listen, and to allow the Holy Spirit to equip us with everything that we need—right down to the details!

QUESTIONS TO CONTEMPLATE

1. Do you, as I do, struggle to surrender your mind, emotions, and will to the Holy Spirit?

2. Now for the tough one: which area are you finding the hardest to surrender? Why do you think that is?

SPACE TO REFLECT

It is a good exercise in "spiritual aerobics" to spend some time actively repenting and turning from any misdeeds of the body, however small, that the Spirit brings to mind. (See Romans 8:13.) Then claim afresh the privilege of being adopted as sons and joint-heirs with Jesus Christ.

A TIME TO PRAY

Lord, I no longer want to be controlled by the sinful nature. Day by day I pray that Your Spirit will equip me to overcome the tactics of the enemy, right down to the last detail. Teach me to surrender my times into Your hands and to surrender every part of myself to You. Please help me to know the freedom of walking with Your Holy Spirit. Amen.

THE PERSON:
WHO COMES TO LIVE IN US

THE VIVID IMAGINATION of George Lucas, the creator of *Star Wars,* could conceive of a vast "force" that might be used to empower us and be employed for either good or evil. This force was personal in that it was available to human personality, but it lacked "personhood" in itself.

That is precisely why the Holy Spirit is different. He is not here for us to employ; we are here for Him to use to bring glory to Jesus through our lives. For this Holy Spirit is not only personal, He also possesses a unique personality. A force would tend to operate by remote control, but the Holy Spirit is just not like that.

God is personal. He neither rules nor communicates by remote control, and He possesses personality. These truths equally apply to the Holy Spirit. Too often we can be tempted to regard the Holy Spirit as some kind of nebulous "force" or a vague divine "it." Nothing could be further from the truth. For God the Father refers to Him as "My Spirit" (Gen. 6:3; Isa. 59:21).

It is to reinforce this point that the apostle John continually refers to the Holy Spirit by using a masculine pronoun (*ekeinos* = he) to accompany a neuter noun (*pneuma* = spirit). This may seem like bad grammar, but it is certainly superb theology! He does this in order to emphasize that the Holy Spirit is a "He," not an "it." (See John 14:26; 15:26; 16:8–14.)

He is the "breath" or "wind" of God (Isa. 40:7). In the New Testament, the Greek word employed is *pneuma*, which literally has those two meanings. It is hard to see how these could be other than broad and vague. Yet Scripture usually brings into grammatical play the definite article. So instead of "*a* breath," or "*a* wind," He is called "*the* Spirit" or "*the* Holy Spirit." His personhood is affirmed in many ways. He can be grieved. He comes upon individuals at particular times. He is the means by which God fills His people, and under exceptional circumstances, He can even be withdrawn from them (Eph. 4:30; Judges 14:6; 2 Kings 2:9; Exod. 35:31; Micah 3:8; Ps. 51:11).

The Holy Spirit is no mere arm or leg of God. He is a Person, and yet

He exists as part of the Godhead. He is not remote but actually indwells God's people. He is, therefore, personal to each one of us. That is the kind of God He is—an up close and personal reality.

THE PERSONALITY OF THE HOLY SPIRIT

Three key characteristics of basic personality lie in our innate capacity for feeling, knowing, and doing. You may be surprised to realize that the Holy Spirit is personally and actively engaged in doing all three!

Scripture affirms that:

⌒He feels (Eph. 4:30).
⌒He knows (John 14:26).
⌒He does (John 16:8–11).

While it is important to note that the Holy Spirit is like us in possessing personality, it is also important to recognize that, unlike us, He is "holy." The Greek word used is *hagios*, and its root meaning is "different." In this sense, He can never be as we are. It is just one demonstration of God's grace and mercy that He allows His "Holy" Spirit to indwell unclean and intrinsically evil human beings. However, it is not just that He is different. The Lord Jesus has given us His Holy Spirit in order that He might make us different, too! The Holy Spirit is at work in attracting people to Jesus, and He is also at work mobilizing us into the same activity.

The very title "Holy Spirit" indicates that this Spirit is totally different to us because He is, in fact, divine. This is true because at the heart of Christian truth lies the conviction that while God is one, He exists as Trinity. (See Matthew 28:19; John 14:26; 15:26; 2 Corinthians 13:14; 1 Peter 1:2.)

In an unusual way, John began his letter to the seven churches in Revelation by greeting them in a manner that places God the Father first, God the Son third, and God the Spirit second (Rev. 1:4–5). While the order might be different, the phraseology is standard because, time and again, the Scriptures refer to the Godhead as three Persons. The implication is inevitable—these three must be regarded as being inextricably intertwined, and they are always coequal together.

GOD IN ACTION

Because we do find it more difficult to visualize and personalize the Holy Spirit, we can often overlook the amount of work in which the Holy Spirit is engaged. It would not be irreverent to say that He is very busy indeed. While He is the corporate Holy Spirit of the universal church (1 Cor. 12:13), He is also the one who indwells the life of every individual believer (Rom. 8:9–11). The Holy Spirit is definitely a multitasker!

The Holy Spirit is constantly at work within our lives to bring us to conviction of sin, recognition of the need for righteousness, and an awareness of impending judgment. All this comes long before a person comes to the point of conversion and surrenders his life to Jesus Christ (John 16:8).

As in the New Testament accounts of the conversions of Zacchaeus, Cornelius, and that unnamed eunuch who was in charge of the treasury for Queen Candace of Ethiopia, the Holy Spirit was actively at work preparing the ground for their moment of truth! In fact, in the latter case, once the Holy Spirit used Philip to explain the Scriptures to the eunuch, He supernaturally transported Philip to Azotus. (See Act 8:26–40.)

When we come to Christ, it is the Holy Spirit who has to take on the "raw material" of the new convert and begin the difficult task, and often lengthy process, of seeking to make each one of us more like our Lord Jesus. (See John 3:5; 2 Corinthians 1:22; Titus 3:5; and especially Romans 8:9–11.)

This whole idea of an indwelling Holy Spirit who inhabits the life of every believer introduced us to a God who could be known, loved, and served right here and now instead of a set of principles or beliefs concerning a god who was "out there" somewhere. We can have a personal relationship with Him.

THOUGHT FOR THE DAY

> Do you not know that your body is a temple of the Holy Spirit, who is in you, whom you have received from God?
>
> —1 CORINTHIANS 6:19

WAIT A MINUTE

It is amazing when we witness the lives of other people being daily influenced by the mighty Spirit of God. It is so easy to just know *about* the Spirit from reading our Bibles, talking to others, and perhaps going to church, but to experience His power and authority at work in our daily lives is another matter entirely.

The living God does desire to live within us. He wants us to keep in step with His Spirit who comes to live within us. He wants to be a personal living reality rather than an ancient uncle whom we rarely visit.

The incredible spiritual breakthrough on the Day of Pentecost inaugurated a whole new dimension of knowing God as a person and marked the beginning of an actual relationship with the living God.

As such, it was the signal for a whole new era. As the Spirit came, power filled the believers' lives (Acts 2). Their fears of being separated from God were shattered, and astonishing grace enabled them to commune with the living God.

The Lord wants each one of us to know Him more and to accept the gift of the Holy Spirit. He did not leave us alone to fight on. He sends His Spirit because He desires to be in a living relationship with every one of us. His Spirit is a person, and people bond, which is the great thrill and privilege into which we are invited to participate today.

Questions to Contemplate

1. Do you *know about* the Holy Spirit, but sometimes struggle to see how His presence is at work in your life each day?

2. Do you sometimes struggle to believe that as a Person, He would want to live in you and use you for His purposes?

Space to Reflect

Consider the fact that this gift has been given to each one of us. Ask the Lord to make His presence "known" in all of our lives that we might be empowered to live in the truth, accepting the Person He has sent.

A Time to Pray

Father, I don't just want to identify with those people who know about Your Holy Spirit. I really desire to see Your presence at work in my life, helping me to grasp how to live completely for You. Amen.

Week 2

DAY 14

THE HELPER:
He Can Make a Difference

One of the single most baffling questions of human history lies in trying to explain how it was that 120 frightened, cowering men and women, barely hanging on to their own existence, could suddenly be transformed into an army of men and women who would effectively turn their world upside down. The answer simply lay in the activity of the Holy Spirit.

One moment they were huddling together for survival; the next they ventured outside their closed walls in order to change the destiny of humankind. Armed with no weapons other than their own naked confidence in the will of God, they persuaded the then "civilized" world to believe their conviction that a dead carpenter was alive and had opened the doors of forgiveness and eternity to all who would surrender the control of their lives into His nail-pierced hands.

Their lives predated the eras of air transportation, information technology, and global communications. Traveling mainly on land, and by foot, progress was frustratingly slow. Regularly they faced the perils of bandits or disease, constantly risking life and limb to the dangers of shipwreck and always knowing that hostile authorities lay at the end of their journey. They were experiencing torture, imprisonment, and death, yet no persecution could extinguish the brightness of their flame. Standing up to proclaim truth in the marketplace, freely gossiping the gospel to colleagues, and entrusting to cumbersome rolls of parchment their message of eternal life painfully but indelibly scratched out by quill, this was no cult that would swiftly die out.

Even death could not exterminate this kind of faith. Far from it, for as the early church historian Tertullian observed, toward the close of the second century A.D., "The blood of the martyrs is the seed of the church."[1]

So how did it happen? What mysterious event took place among people who lived some two thousand years ago in order to usher in a movement that would today incorporate an active membership of more than one million people? No human power could remotely conceive of any means available at that time that could even begin to explain how these events could possibly have happened in the dramatic way that they did. The story almost requires supernatural intervention to become believable. And that is exactly what happened.

HELP FROM OUTSIDE

What they could never have done alone would only have been achieved with support from above. That required a Divine Helper. They were able to set out boldly to go where no one had gone before, because they were now living as those within whose lives the Holy Spirit had taken up permanent residence. Slowly at first, but then accelerating rapidly, they began to seek to win this lost world back for Jesus.

This is exactly what the Holy Spirit does. He makes ordinary people into the very hands and feet of Jesus. This is because of who He is. As God, He is always seeking to shape the lives of God's people and to help us to lift up our heads to appreciate and glory in the full majesty of the Godhead.

Thus it was to begin in a new way at Pentecost. Because Jesus offered Himself on a cross, a new chapter opened in the story of God's dealings with humankind. The Spirit of Jesus would not allow the story to end on a cross or even with an empty tomb. When Jesus cried from a cross the words, "It is finished" (John 19:30), it was far from a scream of defeat—it was a triumphant shout of victory. Death was vanquished, Satan defeated, sin supplanted, and the reign of the kingdom of Jesus inaugurated.

Friday was never intended to be the end, and even Sunday would lead in forty days to Pentecost when the Holy Spirit would take hold of the lives of a group of ordinary people and make them world changers! He began to work at transforming them from what they were into what they could become. The result was to be men and women who, by virtue of the power of the Holy Spirit at work within their lives, had begun to be changed. They were beginning to see God at work both in and through their lives. Contemporary society would soon witness the results and speak with amazement of those "who had turned the world upside down" (Acts 17:6, KJV).

So what, then, is this Holy Spirit helping us to become? He is nothing less than God at work in us, progressively making us to be more and more like Jesus. For this is what the Holy Spirit can accomplish through some very raw material. He takes hold of loads of ordinary people and makes them into those He can use to be responsible for transforming both the history of the world and the population of heaven.

EVEN IN THE BAD TIMES!

It is easy to say that this Holy Spirit is a Person and that He comes to be with us, but what happens when the chips are down? How about when seemingly insuperable problems threaten to overwhelm us? What happens when we are tempted to ask the question where has God gone?

We may glibly pay lip-service to the notion that the Lord always has everything under control and we can place our confidence in Him, but when the rubber meets the road, it is sometimes our fear that rules rather than faith in Him.

The wonderful answer is that even in the middle of the most extreme difficulties we will not be alone, for the Holy Spirit is given to us to be our helper, and He will not leave us to cope alone.

We might want to argue that it would be so much easier if Jesus was actually physically walking alongside of us. We forget that He reminded His disciples, "It is for your good that I am going away. Unless I go away, the Counselor will not come to you; but if I go, I will send him to you" (John 16:7).

In other words, we are not to worry, for help is at hand. This support will not just supply direction, but actually work within us to enable us to arrive at our ultimate destination. But can this Person get us there? Oh, yes, and in case we might ever forget the nature and quality of this aid—our helper is divine!

THOUGHT FOR THE DAY

All of them were filled with the Holy Spirit and began to speak in other tongues as the Spirit enabled them.

—ACTS 2:4

WAIT A MINUTE

The early Christians were not content just to know *about* God; they wanted more. The Holy Spirit was assigned as their "helper," a gift that they desperately needed. He supernaturally helped them to know the Lord Jesus personally and then to begin their mission of taking this good news throughout the world.

The Day of Pentecost marked the day when the early believers received the power of the Spirit enabling them to share the mission of God mightily. This is still the same for us today. God has not stopped equipping

His people; His Spirit is still assigned as our helper to make our mission in Christ's name easier and effective. As Max Anders very helpfully observes, "When we are down, He helps us up. When we need a shove, He gets us moving in the right direction. When we need wisdom, He opens our mind to God's Word. He helps us witness to Jesus both by opening the door of opportunity and by giving us the words to share."[2]

QUESTIONS TO CONTEMPLATE

1. When, and in what ways, have you recently witnessed the Holy Spirit helping you?

2. In that period can you remember a time when you needed a shove in the right direction and He gave you one? What happened?

SPACE TO REFLECT

Remembering that the answers to those questions probably began with a yes, we all need to acknowledge that the Spirit is here as our helper, in which case we need to ask how we might each seek to help others more. The help and support the Spirit supplies are given in order that we might become all the more useful (and usable) in ministering to others!

A TIME TO PRAY

Lord, I pray that You will fill me afresh with the power of Your Spirit, that I may understand afresh Your role as a helper in my life. Amen.

WEEK THREE

THE FIGHT OF OUR LIVES

In Christ they were created (Colossians 1:16) and in Christ they were defeated (Colossians 2:15). Philippians 2:10 makes it quite plain that they must own his sway whether they like it or not. His Lordship, since the resurrection, has been beyond cavil among beings celestial, terrestrial and sub-terranean.

—MICHAEL GREEN
I BELIEVE IN SATAN'S DOWNFALL

There is nothing that Satan more desires than that we should believe that he does not exist and that there is no such place as hell.

—BISHOP WORDSWORTH
SERMON ON FUTURE REWARDS
AND PUNISHMENTS

DAY 15

THE DESERT:
GOD'S LARGE-SCALE SCHOOLROOM

THE THREE YEARS of ministry that were to lie ahead of Jesus were to be the most crucial period in the history of mankind. After this, the world would never be the same again. It was the task of the Holy Spirit to be the teacher of Jesus, to prepare Him for His life of ministry. In exactly the same way, Jesus promised, "the Counselor, the Holy Spirit, whom the Father will send in my name, will teach you all things" (John 14:26). However, a teacher needs a classroom, so the Holy Spirit sent Jesus to His traditional training ground—the desert.

Contrary to what we would like to believe, and sadly have sometimes been taught, the road to spiritual maturity is often not an easy one. Frequently it lies through what many have termed a "wilderness experience." And at times when we are tired, alone, and feeling that we have lost touch with God, Satan sees and seizes his opportunity.

It was in the physical wilderness that the Holy Spirit taught Israel. It was from the desert that God called Moses, in the wilderness that Elijah was recommissioned to his ministry, and in the desert of Arabia that Saul of Tarsus was molded into the apostle Paul.

So it is no surprise that the desert was to be the training ground for John the Baptist. He fulfilled his training so well that Jesus testified of John, "I tell you, among those born of women there is no one greater than John" (Luke 7:28).

Then, tired, hungry, and alone, Jesus faces Satan in the wilderness. But the Holy Spirit Himself had placed Jesus in that position, and it was for a reason! Jesus had thirty years in total obscurity. He emerges from Nazareth, just about the most unlikely place imaginable! He is publicly baptized by John, and at that moment, God the Father speaks from heaven to endorse His Son. At that point of triumph, vindicated before his fellow countrymen, the Holy Spirit drives Jesus into the desert in order that the enemy might tempt Him.

It is easy to ask, "Why? Is this the way God repays faithful service?" Yes, in a way it is. We can often regard a "desert experience" as something

63

purely negative, a period in which we just have to concentrate on survival. But as it was for Jesus, it can so often become God's schoolroom in which the Holy Spirit prepares us for all that lies ahead. It is not when life is easy, but rather when we are going through difficult times, that God will often choose to speak directly to us. After all, Jesus warned us that if we were faithful in small things we would be trusted with bigger matters. God uses that period when we are tested to strengthen and equip us for our Christian life and witness.

FROM TRAGEDY TO TRIUMPH

Satan will always view temptation as an opportunity to score, but time and time again God is simply waiting to reverse our moment of potential tragedy and turn it into one of triumph. But there will always be a cost attached. First of all, Jesus fasted to prepare Himself for the conflict, because some battles can never be won without just that kind of preparation. For the Christian life has never been a glib exercise in what has been called "easy believism" but rather a clear-cut struggle with no less an opponent than the enemy of our souls, Satan.

Even in this kind of situation the Holy Spirit is at work to turn the tables on Satan. For what Satan intended for harm God turns upside down and works it to our benefit. In fact, God often works through our "wilderness experiences" of struggle and hardship in order to bless and direct our lives.

The picture is contained in the minor prophets of a refiner who is hard at work upon a pot of molten gold. He keeps turning the heat up. Every time he increases the temperature, more impurities rise to the surface. He skims them off and removes them to make the gold purer and, therefore, of greater value. Indeed, the refiner will continue to repeat the process until that moment when he can gaze down upon the molten gold and see his own reflection mirrored within it.

The Lord tends to operate in our lives in the same manner. He looks down and reviews all that He could achieve, both in us and through us. Then, while my mind tends to revolt against the idea of a God of love acting as the author of suffering, I do believe that He permits His enemy to throw it at us at times. All this is simply in order that we might be refined in the fire of suffering and opposition, and therefore become more and more like Jesus.

For our God is not just the Lord of the "good times" but of the bad ones as well. It is not in the spiritual "highs," but while we are enduring an arid wilderness experience that God demonstrates to us that His victory over the enemy is a basic part of our spiritual birthright. He trusts us with suffering to teach us that He is always at work through His Holy Spirit taking us away from self-reliance and daily transforming us into all that He wants us to become.

Of course, if Satan had won his conflict with Jesus in the wilderness, then God's plan of redemption would have failed. This was not to be the case because, led by the Spirit, Jesus was ready for him. Nor did Jesus stay in the desert licking His wounds, no. Once the conflict was successfully over, then angels were ready to assist the Son of God to make a swift and total recovery. In boxing terms, it had been victory by a first-round knockout.

THOUGHT FOR THE DAY

Jesus returned to Galilee in the power of the Spirit, and news about him spread through the whole countryside.

—LUKE 4:14

WAIT A MINUTE

We can all go through really tough times, and we can be guilty of blaming God for all that we are going through, when all the while the Spirit is actually molding us more into the likeness of Christ. We find ourselves emerging with greater spiritual maturity, so the Spirit of God can then use us to transform the lives of others. And if we struggle to believe it, then just look at Jesus! He was seriously tempted by the devil, but later His ministry began changing the course of history!

The challenge to us all lies in how we deal with these wilderness times. What we do in the face of adversity will help to determine who we then become. Giving in can have dire and destructive consequences. However, if we are able to cling to the truth and not let go, then we can overcome and, ultimately, become the person God wants us to be.

QUESTIONS TO CONTEMPLATE

1. When was your last "wilderness" experience?

2. What positive difference did it make in your life?

SPACE TO REFLECT

Suppose that you are going through a "valley" right now. Imagine what it would take to allow the Spirit to minister strength and encouragement to you and enable you to hold on in your heart to the truth that you already know in your head. Then contemplate about what you would do, and how you would react differently, if you found yourself facing another wilderness time.

A TIME TO PRAY

Lord, please give me strength when I find myself in the wilderness. Help me to cling to You, to rise above it, and listen to Your truth in the darkness. Amen.

DAY 16

THE TEMPTATIONS:
DEFEATING THE ENEMY

WHAT IS THE Holy Spirit seeking to achieve in our lives? That is a good question, and the answer will not always be obvious. It would be good to both restate and reemphasize the surprising fact that while temptation originates with the enemy of our souls, sometimes he is only acting with divine permission.

The Holy Spirit will often allow the devil to overreach himself by taking hold of our struggles and then employ them to fulfill His own supreme purpose. The unavoidable conclusion is that God allows us to be tempted in order that He may begin to see our lives more perfectly reflecting the love and character of His Son. In other words, His ultimate intention is that each one of us might daily more clearly resemble Jesus.

Where the Holy Spirit observes areas of weakness in our lives, He acts in the same manner as a Peruvian potter. The potter flicks the rim of a pot and listens for the ring that proclaims a perfect glaze. If the sound is wrong, he places the pot back in the oven until the fire has done its work. Only when the tone is perfect will it be passed as a fit vessel for regular usage.

In our own lives, God will highlight our areas of weakness. Israel came under the spotlight of God's own search for living in this same way. Instead of yielding to God's authority and receiving His aid, they failed in their response to temptation, and did so time and time again. That was the reason why, after the Red Sea, they took forty years to complete a two-week journey. God longed to take them into the Promised Land, but the majority ended as bleached bones in the desert.

It can be the same for us. Temptation is not sin. God can use it to mold our lives, but our failure to respond as Jesus intends means that we may have to face going over the same ground for lap after lap, until we finally surrender to His love and authority in our lives. The Holy Spirit will not be content until all those hardened areas of failure and long-continued weaknesses within us have been changed by His love and power.

THE DILEMMA—STONES INTO BREAD

Of the three direct challenges that Jesus faced in the wilderness when receiving the direct assault from Satan, this one must have seemed to be the most straightforward. After a forty-day fast, the Scriptures state the simple fact that "he was hungry" (Luke 4:2). Most of us would have been!

Satan is a specialist in the field of easy answers and offers a simple solution, because he knows that if Jesus simply turns these stones into bread, then Jesus will have misused His divine power by employing it to simply alleviate His own hunger.

A few weeks later Jesus was to feed crowds of four and five thousand with a few loaves and fishes. All He had to do was to advance God's own basic strategy by a matter of weeks, and Jesus could satisfy His own physical needs.

Time and again it is at this level of self-interest that Satan will strike. He will offer anything to keep us complacent and self-indulgent. Satisfy yourself. Enjoy your meetings, books, conferences, records, and friends—just don't exercise spiritual concern for others; save it for yourself. Don't waste your time on the needs of those around you; concentrate on number one. One could even suggest that the temptation would include the desire to satisfy our own spiritual needs, even our own desire to be holy. Anything seems to be acceptable to Satan, if it means that we are content to leave him alone to establish his own area of influence by fostering self-centeredness in our lives.

Now this is directly opposed to those concerns that are prompted by the Holy Spirit in our own lives. He would both instigate and mobilize our efforts to reach out from our spiritual ghettoes into a dying world. Satan, on the other hand, desperately wants to keep us fat, self-interested, relatively content, and at home!

THE DANGER—CHEAP GAINS

Satan's offers of help are usually attractive, and this second one was no exception for Jesus. He is offered His divine legacy of the kingdoms of the world but without the pain of the cross. All He had to do was worship His enemy.

The temptation is to an easy pathway. Satan's gift to Jesus would only, at best, have been temporary. God's legacy to His obedient Son is going to be eternal. In the same way, we face the choice between our own short-lived ambitions or the direction that God has prepared for our lives.

This may involve the inconvenience of moving to live in a less desirable area. It can mean changing jobs or even facing suffering, persecution, or both! Such commitment will seem strange to others in society. As Christians we are faced with a simple choice: bow our knees to Satan for short-term gain, or look to Jesus for an eternal inheritance. As A. W. Tozer so aptly put it, "We can afford to suffer now, we'll have a long eternity to enjoy ourselves."[1]

THE DECEPTION—DESTROY YOURSELF!

Satan knows his Bible and so is good at quoting it out of context. He offered Jesus a shortcut to avoid the cross. He offered an easy route leading to instant popularity. How well he knew that the promise was conditional on the action being in the will of God. How he longed for the body of Jesus to be smashed, spread-eagled on the ground below.

Step outside the will of God, and disaster must be the result. Satan's arguments can be so clever, for he is a better theologian than any of us but remains the devil.

Jesus used two weapons to secure His victory. He stood firm on Scripture and operated in the power of the Holy Spirit. He repeats that "it is written," and the word of God proceeds from the Holy Spirit. As Paul said, "The Holy Spirit spoke the truth to your forefathers when he said through Isaiah" (Acts 28:25).

It is as we spend time reading God's Word that the Holy Spirit can lead us not only to understand the truth but also to live the truth. The Holy Spirit is holy and cannot tolerate sin. So His power is always available to keep us separate from Satan's superficial offers. It is so reassuring to know that it is this "Spirit of holiness" (Rom. 1:4) who is the One that God has placed within us in order that we may stand and grow in Him.

BETTER LUCK NEXT TIME

"When the devil had finished all this tempting, he left him until an opportune time" (Luke 4:13). Having led Him into the wilderness, the Holy Spirit had initiated a vital process in the life of Jesus. He had triumphed and not just in one encounter. The devil would be back to try again, but now an ongoing narrative of victory over Satan had been established. The anointing of the Spirit at Jesus' baptism proved to be real. Jesus entered the wilderness "full of the Spirit," and triumphing over Satan, He "returned to Galilee in the power of the Spirit" (Luke 4:14). It was fullness that led to power. The result was a defeated Satan, and the years of triumph had begun.

But we too will face temptations that can certainly parallel those endured by Jesus. These can be summarized as the temptation to whine (to bemoan our physical condition), to shine (to be content to flare up for an instant of superficial popularity or acceptance), or to recline (to take the easy way out). None of these options are good enough for God. They were not good enough for Jesus, and so neither should they be for us.

But Jesus gained the victory alone; we don't have to. He gives us the strength with which to win the battle. The reason is because Jesus had been completely victorious on a cross, and because we too know that same Holy Spirit, there is an inescapable conclusion. By living in obedience to the will of Jesus for our lives and through the power of His Spirit within us, we also will enjoy victory over the powers, ways, and deceptions of the devil.

We too can, and will, defeat the enemy.

THOUGHT FOR THE DAY

When the devil had finished all this tempting, he left him until an opportune time.

—LUKE 4:13

WAIT A MINUTE

How we respond to temptation is very important. Temptation is not sin in itself, but it does demand a response from us. When it begins to nag away at us, we must refrain from giving in to its power. Instead we should tackle it head on, asking the Spirit of God to help us. If we do not deal with it quickly, it will often lead to sin. If it doesn't evoke us to sin soon, it will keep coming back to haunt us over and over again. The devil desperately doesn't want us to overcome his tactics, so he tries different ways of tempting us over the same issue. He will "dress up" the sin with a variety of tempting offers to see which one causes us to succumb. He works out where we are weak and will attack these areas frequently.

However, the Spirit of God lives in us, and He is stronger than the spirit of darkness. If we ask Him, the Spirit can strengthen us to recognize the attacks and overcome them, so that we can be free from particular struggles. David gave into temptation and slept with Bathsheba, leading to terrible consequences (2 Sam. 11). He blocked out the Word of the Lord, probably knowing his actions were displeasing to the Lord (v. 27). The

Spirit of holiness (Rom. 1:4) provides a way out, but He does require that we submit to His love and authority, however weak we might feel. For in Him lies the ultimate victory.

QUESTIONS TO CONTEMPLATE

1. Has there been something in your life that keeps surfacing and you need to deal with it once and for all?

2. Is there anything tempting you right now with which you need to confront?

SPACE TO REFLECT

The Spirit of God is the only way you can overcome the temptations. Why don't we consider "putting on the armor" each day (Eph. 6:10ff), so that His prompting becomes clearer?

A TIME TO PRAY

Lord, I recognize that I am involved in a spiritual battle. Please give me the strength of Your Holy Spirit to overcome the temptations that keep trying to cripple me. Thank You that while Satan knows those arguments that undermine me, in You always lies the final victory. Amen.

Day 17

The Enemy Is Not All That He's Cracked Up to Be

SOME CHRISTIANS SEEM to manage to live most of their spiritual lives in blissful ignorance of the devil's very existence. The reason lies in the fact that because they never trouble him, he rarely needs to bother them!

Once we begin to show an interest in being totally committed to God and living in the power of the Holy Spirit, then that is the moment for Satan to start to worry! For he fears the conflict and exposure that may result when he is exposed to the light.

The devil far prefers the darkness and appreciates the immunity and protection that it gives him. He hates to be challenged, because he fears those who might wake up and stand against him. The plain and simple fact is that he really is a coward at heart.

These statements may sound surprising, but the reason for them is best understood when we begin to recognize who he really is and contrast his very limited power and personality with that of the Holy Spirit.

1. Satan is a defeated opponent. In the first place he was only a created being. He possesses more of the attributes of humankind than of the divine, for he employs violence in order to achieve his objectives. He is a liar, a deceiver, and one who gets it wrong!

One thing he could not tolerate was God's Son bringing salvation and freedom to ordinary men and women. He set out to frustrate God's purposes, but instead he ended up doing the very things that were necessary to accomplish them.

2. Satan is the victim of a major disadvantage. His pride makes him try to compete in the wrong league. He is only a created being who was expelled from heaven for seeking to oppose God. As such he can never aspire to be a true opponent for the Holy Spirit. What is more, Satan knows it and fears!

3. Satan is limited in time and space. He can only be in one place at a time. The Holy Spirit, on the other hand, can be everywhere at the same time. Satan is terribly limited and has to employ an army of demon spirits to move at his command. For this reason one is very unlikely to have a personal encounter with Satan. His activities are both temporary and localized. What a contrast to the Holy Spirit who comes to live inside the people of God all day long.

4. Satan's bitterness and anger are so fierce that he has engaged in violent actions against those who have given direction of their lives to the Holy Spirit. The response that the devil wants to make toward Spirit-filled lives resembles the attitude displayed in a warning sign outside a Beverly Hills house: "Warning—Trespassers will be shot. Survivors will be prosecuted."

Satan tried through every means at his disposal to make us afraid of the Holy Spirit, leading us to see Him as a cause of division rather than unity. The devil's strategy was brilliantly simple—he tried to make us either feel arrogant because of some experience we had or inferior because we lacked it!

For years our spiritual insecurities can make us far too easy a prey for him. We seem to be so afraid that others will be ahead of us in the race, that instead of rejoicing at the way God leads them, we insist that they come back to join us on our own spiritual pathway.

AN INFERIOR OPPONENT?

In this serious exercise of spiritual warfare, it is of vital importance to notice that we are not merely engaged in a series of conflicts with wrong habits or ideas, but with an actual and personal enemy who represents spiritual reality at its very worst.

For this reason Satan can never be simply dismissed as an irrational fear or as a joke. Yet, although this enemy is to be treated with respect, he is not to be regarded as an all-powerful one to be treated with dread. Scripture is quite insistent that while this is a personal devil, he is not comparable for a single moment with God. Satan is a strong and persuasive opponent, but he is one who is ready and waiting to be conquered. For the victory over this enemy has already been won on our behalf.

We really do have nothing to be afraid of apart from our obedience to our Father God and the way in which we are seeking to do His will. This point is made no less than 366 times in the Bible as we are repeatedly given the instruction and reassurance, "Don't be afraid." In other words, we have nothing to fear.

So why are these comforting words repeated so often? Well, it is one for every day of the year, and an extra one for leap years. The need to go on and on making the point comes from the fact that this is one truth that is absolutely essential for each one of us to take hold of. The reason for this repetition is undoubtedly because we tend to be slow learners.

This is why Jesus taught His disciples to pray that they would not fall into temptation and that they would be preserved from the onslaughts of the evil one. He did this because He won the first skirmish with Satan in the wilderness and then the ultimate triumph on the cross. Through the triumph of crucified love, He inaugurated a wonderful new life through His death. This once-and-for-all sacrifice was to be the turning point of history; the power of darkness was forever gloriously exterminated in the light of an empty tomb.

A new era had dawned, and the day of the Holy Spirit had arrived. Now the possibility of living in a new dimension of life had become a vivid reality.

THOUGHT FOR THE DAY

> Be self-controlled and alert. Your enemy the devil prowls around like a roaring lion looking for someone to devour. Resist him, standing firm in the faith because you know that your brothers throughout the world are undergoing the same kind of suffering.
>
> —1 PETER 5:8–9

WAIT A MINUTE

It is healthy for us to consider who our enemy really is. If you think about it, it would be crazy for soldiers to go into battle without considering what they are up against! Every time there is a battle of sorts, both sides assess what their opponents are capable of. If they went blindly in to fight, most would be defeated instantly. As a commander not only do you have to look at the enemy, but you also have to think about how, when, and where they will choose to strike you. And so it is with our spiritual enemy; we need to acknowledge who he is and where our weaknesses lie. When we identify them, we are able to take our stand against his schemes in a much more productive way.

QUESTIONS TO CONTEMPLATE

1. Have you considered "who" Satan really is before now?

2. Does reading more about him help you to understand his tactics and how to take a better "stand"?

SPACE TO REFLECT

Ask yourself: *Have I thought about the devil's strategies? If not, how much or how little do I think I need to get a grasp on his role?*

A TIME TO PRAY

Lord, thank You that You have all power and authority over this universe. Thank You that the enemy is defeated. Help me not to allow him any ground in my life and to recognize when he is at work. Amen.

THE SECULARIST:
Living in Denial

TODAY WE LIVE in an interesting culture of contradictions. On the one hand, there is an absolute obsession and dependency on materialism and the physical realm. But on the other, there is an acceptance of a spiritual dimension in the form of astrology, eastern religion, occultism, and new cults. We live in a world that has an all-absorbing fascination with the unknown, along with an equal determination to avoid giving it too much substance or acknowledgment.

The problem for Christians who do not want to remain silent about their faith lies in knowing how to begin to attempt to convince a world that is so totally obsessed by materialism and physical realities as ours that there really is another dimension to life. Related to this is the fact that, in seeing the material as an independent reality, we fail to recognize that spiritual powers can often be the invisible pianist playing upon a very visible piano.

The Gods of Our Age?

While many believe that there are no divine or supernatural forces in existence in the universe, they are forced to concede that there are many things that, frankly, we do not understand. We begin to recognize that there is just too much around that simply defies the human imagination. It has been quite easy to affirm that when a car breaks down this is more likely to be due to a mechanical fault than mischievous jinn that need to be cast out of the machinery. However, the results of a private séance or the exercise of astral projection often lie outside the realm of rational explanation. The same applies to a variety of overseas phenomena like the practice of voodoo in Haiti or activities associated with the spirit world in African tribal religions.

It may be popular to consider the concept of "the powers" as the product of a simple-minded person's imagination or relegate them to the level of myths, but then become so fascinated with the unknown. Contemporary France, for example, as the epitome of a modern materialistic society has more psychic mediums per head of population than any other Western nation.

Our lives are full of unanswered questions. These would tend to include problem areas such as:

- What follows death?
- Why do each tribe and culture select something or someone to worship?
- Where does our human creativity come from?
- When will I understand the human inner personal desire to uncover the transcendent to find something "out there"?

Questions like these defy our desire for easy answers. There is only one answer: God has come to our world—in a person—in order that He might reveal His reality to us! This answer is personal and concrete—the other alternatives rest on a vivid imagination or mere human theory.

THOUGHT FOR THE DAY

This is my own dear Son—listen to Him.

—MARK 9:7, GNT

WAIT A MINUTE

What is absent today is a true understanding of the spiritual realm that is controlled by the Godhead, who is ultimately Lord over all the earth!

Consequently many have been content to settle down into their material lives with added spiritual extras that happen to "work for them." And the attitude pervades that "what works for me may not work for you!" It is into this climate that we try to convey that Jesus is *the* way, *the* truth, and *the* life (John 14:6).

The spiritual ideas that people have begun to practice are sought after to satisfy needs that are not met by the material world. They can change, evolve, and be added to at any time. What is strange is that the two—spiritual and secular—do not combine on every level, and so you find people who are quick to assert that a car breaking down is more likely due to a mechanical fault than a demon needing to be cast out of the machinery! We have to share Christ in this Western world without separating Him from any aspect of our worldview and without limiting Him to only being *a way*. But that would be the majority's preference!

QUESTIONS TO CONTEMPLATE

1. In a Western world with these issues, how can you help people to distinguish between supernatural reality and what is only bogus or counterfeit?

2. How do you express the exclusive claims of Jesus to a postmodern world where "anything goes" without being rejected as mindless, fanatical, or too extreme?

SPACE TO REFLECT

Praise God that we don't have to argue people into the kingdom, that we have the Spirit of God equipping us to share Jesus in our society, and that He does the convicting and convincing!

A TIME TO PRAY

Lord, help me to share You in a world looking for answers in all the wrong places. Please equip me with the power of Your Spirit to recognize that I am engaged in a spiritual battle, affecting every area of my life, and to declare real spiritual truth to people who have only found temporary answers. Amen.

Day 19

THE POWERS:
Beware, Enemy Forces in Operation

THE PROBLEM WITH having to live in a world where we are faced with so many unanswered questions and unexplained mysteries is that we are left with so many gaps in our understanding. We have left plenty of room for fantasy and superstition to complement what was already a thoroughly corrupt picture. Today around 140 million people follow various forms of primal religion. Each one commonly presents a society as being populated by invisible powers that permeate the whole of human life and existence.

Such unseen powers are frequently viewed as attaching themselves to ancestors, mythological heroes, inanimate objects such as trees and flowers, or even to the wider forces of nature. A concern for the personal welfare and well-being of the community means that such "forces" must inevitably be "appeased" or kept happy. They are regarded as conferring personal safety, success, and failure and must be constantly cared for in order to placate them and prevent them from bringing harm to family, wealth, or friends.

The use of magic and ritual, often facilitated by specialists such as pagan priests or witch doctors, is usually viewed as an essential part of life. Many view ancestor worship as being essential. It is only by such means that protection can be acquired against the mischievous activities of malevolent spirits. We may find it easy to joke about such beliefs, but their influence remains strong in many societies—and with very negative results.

This is why the whole concept of the powers is so difficult to understand, and because we cannot devise a neat little box in which to place them we can be guilty of ignoring them. For the Bible does not present us with tidy distinctions in relation to unseen spirits. Scripture sees the physical and spiritual as being often intermingled and presents us with many vivid pictures of forces that are at work in our world—forces that are clearly beyond our human control.

These forces are not merely powerful. The ways in which they are described often amount to little less than a definition of power itself. Words that the Bible employs about them include names like "principalities," "powers," and "thrones." These clearly refer to superhuman powers (Rom. 8:38; Eph. 6:12; Col. 1:16; 2:15), and yet the same words are used elsewhere to describe human rulers (Luke 12:11; Acts 4:26). On other occasions the distinction in Scripture is even less clear, and these words could describe either human or supernatural forces (Rom. 13:1; 1 Cor. 2:8; Titus 3:1).

Once we have come to acknowledge that powerful spiritual realities exist beyond ourselves, then to see a diabolic strategy behind these awful deeds can scarcely be regarded as blind fantasy. We all need to face up to the fact that Scripture does warn us of the reality that "the god of this age has blinded...minds" (2 Cor. 4:4).

Danger—Powers at Play

Where are these powers? The Bible declares that they are all around us. It refers to angels of light (Ps. 91:11; Matt. 4:6; Heb. 1:4–7) and to that myriad of angels that chose to follow Satan in his rebellion against God and form the nucleus of his demon forces (Matt. 12:22–29; Luke 8:30–38; Rev. 16:13–14).

These demons may attach themselves to specific territories or practices (Daniel 10:13; 12:1ff). They appear to be equally at home in "the pit" (Luke 8:31; Rev. 1:9–11), which is probably where we would expect to find them, or in "the air" (Eph. 2:2), from which strategic vantage point they are ready and able to harass humankind. These conquered satanic powers have yet to be tamed and domesticated. While they have no choice but to acknowledge the victory of Jesus over them, they still remain in a state of active rebellion against Him (Phil. 2:10). Now their ultimate defeat has already been secured through the power of crucified love, but we need to be on the alert because they will continue to attempt to exercise their pervasive influence over structures and individuals alike.

All around the world there are particular countries that, in recent years, have managed to either attract or repel their wealthier neighbors—and with significant results. But to attribute the reasons for the growth or decline of a nation to purely political or economic factors alone may mean that we are in danger of missing the point!

Haiti would provide us with a good illustration. Only thirty years ago, when compared to the neighboring Dominican Republic, Haiti's future looked bright. Today that has changed. Her once burgeoning tourist industry has collapsed in ruins, and whole sections of her economy appear to be shattered. Occasionally attempts are made to change things, but skepticism is the normal response for any claims that Haiti is now a budding and emergent democracy.

The main reason is that corruption still seems to rule as confidently as ever. As far as violence goes, it is certainly not safe to walk the streets alone at night. One time my youngest daughter, Suzy, was being chauffeured through the streets of Port-au-Prince, when the vehicle passed a man who had just been murdered. And it was only around midday!

On another day I walked out of filming a section of one of Haiti's quasi-voodoo ceremonies. This was specially designed for the more adventurous type of tourist with a hunger for the more bizarre side of life, but I felt repelled by what I had just witnessed. The feelings of disgust did not simply come because here was a mature Westerner who knew that all of this was fake. Instead I was nauseated because these things offered a pale imitation of real spiritual powers whose shadows have dominated Haiti for so long.

The camera crew joined me as we made our way down toward one of Haiti's largest churches. I stood outside and simply explained to the camera that I am an Englishman, and I come from a country that had many of its origins in witchcraft. I certainly have no difficulty believing in the existence of the devil. We interviewed a former voodoo priest who had met Jesus and rejected all of his former practices. Reflecting on what he had said, I knew that, like him, I may be convinced about Satan's existence, but I am even more convinced when I say, "I believe in Satan's downfall."

As I tried to explain this truth that day, it suddenly finally dawned on me that the real problem for Haiti did not ultimately lie in its form of government, its economy, its corruption, or its incipient violence. These were only symptoms rather than the real cause. For the spiritual darkness that pervaded Haiti has negatively influenced every area of its national life. That is why the Haitian churches have now begun to take action against voodoo practices and those plaguing powers that have permeated society, and today they are seeking to redirect their nation toward Jesus Christ.

THOUGHT FOR THE DAY

For I am convinced that neither death nor life, neither angels nor demons, neither the present nor the future, nor any powers, neither height nor depth, nor anything else in all creation, will be able to separate us from the love of God that is in Christ Jesus our Lord.

—ROMANS 8:38–39

WAIT A MINUTE

One woman recently admitted that she used to be a practicing witch. She said she would always know when she saw a Christian because they would have a "glow" about them. She told one of our friends, "You don't realize the power that you Christians have!" How true! This woman was aware of the Spirit of God shining through the life of the believer.

Too often we separate the physical aspects of our world from the spiritual when actually the Bible is clear that the two are intermingled. The danger is, then, that we do not see the world through the eyes that God intended us to use, for what is invisible to us is seen only too clearly by Him. Realizing and recognizing the reality of the spiritual realm will enable us to utilize the gifts of the Spirit to make a difference for Christ. This will help us to engage with people on a much deeper level, making a greater impact for the kingdom of God.

QUESTIONS TO CONTEMPLATE

1. Read Psalm 91:11; Matthew 4:6; Luke 8:30–39; Colossians 1:16; 2:15; Ephesians 2:2; and Hebrews 1:4–7. How aware would you say you are of this spiritual realm and the powers that operate within it?

2. Jesus has triumphed over all. How can you better live in the victory that He intended?

3. Does your worldview need changing?

SPACE TO REFLECT

Together let us ask the Lord to open our eyes to see the world from His perspective and enable us to join in the conflict by moving ahead in the power of His Spirit.

A TIME TO PRAY

Father, forgive me for not living in the reality of a world with a spiritual realm and for separating my physical life from the spiritual one that You intended. Help me to live in the fullness of Your gospel, grasping what we are up against, and who is for us! Amen.

THE BATTLE:
Spiritual Warfare for Beginners

One act of which most of us would probably wish to remain in a state of blissful ignorance is that the Holy Spirit does not normally go into battle alone. We would prefer that the fight did not actually involve us! The uncomfortable fact is that the Holy Spirit usually enters into combat with enemy powers by working in and through the people of God. In other words, we are quite likely to find ourselves on the front line!

Of course, when it comes to cosmic warfare, most of us are cowards at heart. We might well wish that we were simply not involved. But the truth of the matter is that we were not recruited into the armies of the living God in order to engage in civilian pursuits. However unpleasant it may seem, the fact is that sometimes God intends His people to go to war, but at such moments He does specifically arm them with superior power, with the might and majesty of His Holy Spirit.

It is significant to note that the apostle Paul instructs us to "put on the full armor of God" (Eph. 6:13) and be prepared for battle. But none of the armor that God has provided is designed to protect our backs. It all operates on the assumption that we will always be moving forward. Neither defeat nor retreat is considered an option. We are called upon to stand as the army of God marching together under divine direction to share in the triumph of Jesus over Satan and the Holy Spirit's victory over the powers.

The reason for our boldness lies in the sense of security that we have found in knowing that the one sure antidote against Satan and his legions of angels lies in the blood of Jesus Christ and the power of His Holy Spirit. It is here that true spiritual authority can be found and experienced. So while we might have wished that we could remain as spiritual pacifists, at least we can know that we are on the winning side.

IGNORANCE OF THE DEVIL

In any battle the first necessity is that we know our enemy. In a society that is generally skeptical about even the devil's existence, this is not an easy task. While "talk of the devil" is one of those phrases that just slips off the tongue, there are few of us who ever give serious thought to the words that we are using. Tragically the very idea of a personal devil is enough to cause many to break out into guffaws of laughter.

Yet it is strange to note that these very same folks find nothing strange in accepting the necessity for avoiding ladders, touching wood, or even "kissing the blarney stone." We do appear to be quite happy with what falls within our comfort zones or can provide us with further entertainment value. But the concept of a personalized demonic architect of evil—Satan himself—no way.

We live in a confused world. On the one hand people are searching for truth in New Age principles, and on the other hand they are living dependent on all things that will pass away eventually. Whatever their worldview, we know that we are engaged in a real spiritual battle with real powers at work in our dark world. We cannot deny that we are called upon by our Lord Jesus to join in Satan's defeat.

So how on earth can that be accomplished? While there certainly are things that we can do, there are areas that only God can handle, and, therefore, we are called upon to pray strongly, vigorously, and continuously. Because the powers are evil, we must look and pray to the one who is good in order that their strategies might be thwarted.

PRAYER THAT CHANGES THE WORLD

We are not only called on to recognize our enemy's existence but to participate in the battle against him. To that end, we are called upon to pray. The reason is that if we are to engage in effective spiritual warfare in this way, then we will not achieve it on our own. We will need the Holy Spirit's enabling if we are to pray effectively. Scripture does place all of our spiritual abilities and resources in the simple context of our learning how to "pray in the Spirit on all occasions" (Eph. 6:18).

Often I think that our failure to recognize the existence of supernatural forces is only equaled by our failure to recognize the power that is available to us in prayer.

It is a fair question to ask as to whether major world events like wars, man-made disasters, famine, civil unrest, and many others might have happened differently—or even have been avoided—if only the church had risen up to face her God-given challenge of interceding on behalf of others. If we had learned what it means to accept the responsibility of praying constantly in the Holy Spirit, then what would the God of heaven have accomplished on the earth? One has to really wonder at what God would do in response to His church praying in this way.

It is only as we pray that we can unlock the gates of heaven and see the living God release His grace and power upon us again. It is not sufficient for us to be content with murmuring a routine or ritual prayer on behalf of those in government. Paul insisted that high-level spiritual warfare should be a reality in our spiritual experience (Eph. 6:12). Jesus pointed out that a successful invasion of opposition territory is dependent upon our first being able to bind and immobilize the strong man (Matt. 12:24–29). That is exactly what happens when we start to pray strong prayers. It would be naïve to think that we could ever see the rooting out of injustice and victory over the powers by any other means.

We will only be able to see evil powers defeated when we engage in that regular and rigorous activity of committed intercession that is a part of the way that God always intended us to pray. Whenever injustice is faced in the world as the result of the powers being at work, then the measure of our concern for the poor and the powerless can be seen, not just in the level of our giving or through our personal involvement, but in how we pray.

For whenever Satan uses his minions to seek to frustrate the work of God, then prayer is the immediate and appropriate defense in the face of enemy attack. When the powers strike, then we are called to strike back. The Holy Spirit not only keeps us from defeat and death, but He then uses us to give life to others. This is what prayer does, and it is great to be able to witness the lives of so many people around the world being transformed both physically and spiritually through the care and support of the churches and the love of God's people around the world. Yet the enemy still does try to interfere, and naturally enough one of his prime targets will always be those strategic occasions when decisions taken will determine the future direction of God's work.

We are not called to run away from spiritual conflict or to ignore the plight of those for whom the very survival of themselves and their families is at risk on a daily basis. Instead we are called upon to follow in the footsteps of that one who demonstrated that the very opposite of satanic power can be seen in a baby laid in a manger and a man dying unjustly on a cross. His life supremely showed that compassion toward others, and it showed the sense of prayerful dependence on His Father that caused the powers to shudder.

Whatever the powers may seek to throw at us, we must follow His example. It is in order that we may live our lives for Jesus that the Holy Spirit is constantly equipping us. It is He who encourages us, empowers us, equips us, and enables us to successfully take on every enemy. It is the Holy Spirit who will give us victory in the battle; it is only our task to take our stand in His service.

THOUGHT FOR THE DAY

For our struggle is not against flesh and blood, but against the rulers, against the authorities, against the powers of this dark world and against the spiritual forces of evil in the heavenly realms.

—EPHESIANS 6:12

WAIT A MINUTE

If we identify the fact that our "struggle" is not against flesh and blood, but is a "spiritual struggle," then we need a spiritual response. Prayer aids us in our struggle. If we are literally in a battle, the prayers that we pray need to be constant, consistent, and powerful.

So often we go about our daily life as if what we do is inconsequential. We go into meetings and make various decisions and changes to our job world, and we think nothing of it. We are oblivious to the power of prayer. It not only thwarts the enemy's plans, but it also increases our chances of making a greater difference for the Lord. Prayer recognizes the Spirit of God at work in us and through us and the fact that it can and will change circumstances and situations dramatically. We will not get half as far or achieve half of what we could if we are not engaged in prayer.

QUESTIONS TO CONTEMPLATE

1. In what particular circumstances can you pray more effectively?

2. How does your knowledge of the enemy's tactics change the way you will pray?

3. How can you involve powerful prayer more in your daily life?

SPACE TO REFLECT

Consider whom you might encourage to pray with you or as well.

A TIME TO PRAY

Lord, thank You that we do not go into the struggle alone and engage with the spiritual forces of evil by ourselves. We praise You that we have the powerful tool of prayer to equip us to fight effectively and see You make a difference through us. Amen.

THE VICTORS:
IN A TRIAL OF STRENGTH

*I*NEVER ANTICIPATED the reception that I was to receive at one village in Mozambique. Frankly, I was a little embarrassed to receive a hero's welcome upon entering a village that I had never visited before. It was only when the tribal elders explained it was Mozambican women staff members who had earned this honor for me that I began to understand. The more questions I asked, the more the story slowly began to unfold.

To appreciate the story, you need to know a little about the pagan and cultural heritage of this tribe. Linda Ngzane, an African nurse on our staff, had begun to operate a child survival program for World Relief in that part of the country.

When she visited this particular village, she discovered that a high percentage of children under five years of age were dying from diarrhea. The people simply accepted this as a fact of life. It was a problem that had been with them for decades. Whenever a child fell sick they followed the instructions the witch doctors had given them. A bowl of water would be placed outside the family's hut and a damp cloth would be used to wipe the child's bottom. Afterward, the cloth was placed in the bowl of water. The process was repeated after each bout of diarrhea. Every night a portion of the water from the bowl was carefully measured out, diluted, and then given to the child to drink. The bowl of water was retained overnight, and the next morning this routine would continue. Eventually the baby or young child would be reduced to being forced to drink barely diluted diarrhea. The inevitable result was that many of them died.

Linda became quite desperate because this practice had traditionally received the backing of the tribal elders. Few would have dared to defy the witch doctor's instructions. Patiently, Linda worked to convince the mothers that this was all wrong. Eventually she succeeded; the bowl of diarrhea became replaced by a simple salt solution, and the children began to survive. This undermined the witch doctors, and their influence diminished because the people became more open to different spiritual answers.

Perhaps it is not surprising that today there are nearly 150,000 Mozambican young people from that area who are meeting weekly in Bible studies seeking to learn how to love and serve Jesus Christ.

The question remains as to who on earth would have originated such a vile and evil way of doing things? Was it pure ignorance, or did more malevolent forces play their own part in creating this tragedy?

THE DECISIVE FACTOR

Sadly, many of us are strangely silent when it comes to issues relating to the reality of the Holy Spirit. As has already been pointed out, it is a sad fact that throughout church history, theologians have seemed less confident in talking about God the Holy Spirit than they have about either the Father or the Son. We have failed to recognize what should be an unmistakable fact—too often in our lives and battles, as in those of Jesus, the Holy Spirit is intended to be the decisive factor.

But the harsh notes of controversy have too often dogged the activities of the Holy Spirit. We have failed to understand both who He is and how He operates. Continually people have objected to claims of His activity by responding that God cannot work in this way or the other. Certainly it is true that we tend to feel safer with the activities of God the Father, revealed in creation, or the Son as we see Him in Jesus. The dominant activities of the Holy Spirit lie in the here and now, and that can appear to be far more unsettling, even dangerous. We feel safer looking backwards into the past than we do in experiencing God's power in our lives in the present. But to tell the living God how He may or may not work is the height of human presumption and could be a very dangerous practice indeed.

It is true that human energy and endeavor remain far more easily managed and accounted for than the unpredictable, and sometimes dramatic, interventions from God the Holy Spirit. But just because He operates outside, our own determination can scarcely provide adequate grounds for the exclusion of the Holy Spirit from our plans and actions. After all, Jesus promised His disciples that they would not have to struggle on in their own energies: "I will not leave you as orphans; I will come to you" (John 14:18).

So the major difficulty that confronts us is that, whatever we may wish to think, each and everyone of us is incapable of living the life of God without the power of the Holy Spirit. As Paul wrote, "Even though the desire to do good is in me, I am not able to do it" (Rom. 7:18, GNT). But the amazing news is that God has not abandoned us to this problem. He has not left us to somehow struggle on trying to survive alone. Rather than being neglected orphans, we are the proud possessors of God's Holy Spirit. It is incredibly easy to forget that this Spirit is the Holy Spirit. He expects us to be holy, too, and works in our lives to bring that about. But that will inevitably bring us in direct opposition with Satan himself.

Victory is available, right here and now. It comes through crucified love and the blood that was spilt from a cross, then the power to live in the good of that triumph comes directly from the Holy Spirit. This great victory was not won over some vague, impersonal force of evil. Jesus taught His disciples to pray for victory and deliverance in their battle with an "evil one." That is a much better translation from the original Greek text, for he is not some vague nebulous force but a very real and active opponent.

Jesus knew that full and total victory over him was freely available, but even He could only face life on earth in opposition to the will of Satan through the power of the Holy Spirit. So that power was given to Him. As soon as Jesus was baptized, the Holy Spirit filled Him. "He saw the Spirit of God coming down like a dove and lighting on him" (Matt. 3:16, GNT).

It was from a cross that Jesus made a public example of Satan and his powers. He unmasked these hidden forces as enemies of the living God and demonstrated that while the Roman system of justice and the Jewish religious structures were merely puppets of powers more mighty than themselves, Jesus could reign over them from a tree.

It was through crucified love that Jesus triumphed over the enemy. Then in His resurrection, by the Holy Spirit, He penetrated and captured the enemy's territory. Jesus had successfully invaded the realm of destruction and death and inflicted a resounding and total defeat upon the principalities and powers on their own ground.

None of this could ever have been possible apart from the cross. Only there could divine forgiveness meet the requirements of divine holiness. On a cross, heaven's love and justice met—and embraced. Now the Spirit could come to forgiven lives. Now God's purposes would be fulfilled among the Gentiles. Now the church would emerge as a covenant people of God. Now the good news of saving faith in Jesus would spread throughout the earth. Motivated by His love for humankind and supremely by His desire to do His Father's will, Jesus paid the price of our sins. On a cross, He died out of love for us.

This single event clearly and finally initiated Satan's downfall. Now no one could ever doubt this one single and gloriously liberating truth—our enemy has been defeated!

THOUGHT FOR THE DAY

Finally, be strong in the Lord and in his mighty power. Put on the full armor of God so that you can take your stand against the devil's schemes.

—EPHESIANS 6:10–11

WAIT A MINUTE

An old hymn insisted that we should, "Stand up, stand up for Jesus, ye soldiers of the cross."[1] As Christians if we fail to take this challenge seriously, then we are in danger of making little difference to the kingdom of God.

Thankfully we have been given the Spirit of the Lord to equip us to make a valid response. We are called to put on the "full armor of God so that we can take our stand against the devil's schemes." Metaphorically, "putting on the armor" helps us to take a stand against all things seen and unseen, and the Spirit's prompt suddenly seems clearer to us. Praying in the Spirit on all occasions (Eph. 6:18) is another means of response to the battle that we are engaged in. Prayer is a powerful weapon that enables us to commune with the living Lord, impacting heaven with intercession that can affect things dramatically.

QUESTIONS TO CONTEMPLATE

1. Have you equipped yourself with the armor of God today?

2. In which case are you praying effectively: asking God that you might minister in His power, knowing His protection, and ultimately allowing Him to change the lives of other people through you?

SPACE TO REFLECT

We need to allow God to equip us with all that we need to "take our stand" for Him each day.

A TIME TO PRAY

Lord Jesus, I recognize that I am engaged in a real fight! But I am not alone, and I am on the winning side! Help me to take my stand, together with my brothers and sisters, to impact this earth for You. Amen.

WEEK FOUR

SUPERNATURAL LIVING

[He makes] his ministers a flame of fire, am I ignitable? God deliver me from the dread asbestos of "other things." Saturate me with the oil of the Spirit, that I may be aflame.

—JIM ELLIOTT

The popular notion that the first obligation of the church is to spread the gospel to the uttermost parts of the earth is false. Her first obligation is to be spiritually worthy to spread it. Our Lord said, "Go ye," but he also said, "Tarry ye," and the tarrying had to come before the going. Had the disciples gone forth as missionaries before the day of Pentecost it would have been an overwhelming spiritual disaster, for they could have done no more than make converts after their own likeness.

—A. W. TOZER

THE SEARCH:
LOOKING FOR THE PROMISE

I NOW KNOW that I was not alone when, as a relatively young Christian, I first began to question what the reason could be for the inadequacies and failures in much of my Christian experience.

I knew that, in theory at least, Satan had been defeated, but often I felt that I was, too! I well remember that time because I was so deeply troubled at the poverty of my own spiritual walk with God. So much of what I knew appeared to come as information "about" God rather than a direct relationship with Him. I had to ask why my actions so frequently failed to match up to my words.

I remember only too well how my heart used to open up with longing when I read spiritual writers like A. W. Tozer who wrote of what it meant to know God "other than by hearsay." But I was riddled with doubts as to what it would mean to move on with God, and if the answers were what I feared they might be, then was I prepared to go there?

I began to ask why it was that so many other Christians seemed to know so much more of the indwelling love of Jesus than I did. I could not help but wonder why it was that their lives seemed to display the fruits of His grace and demonstrate the power of God in ways that it seemed that I failed to do. I began to doubt that my Christian life was all that it should be.

However, I was soon to discover that I was not the only one who had encountered this kind of frustration. In fact, I became even more amazed to discover there were many others who felt the same way I did!

At a personal level the biggest struggle that I faced as a young Christian lay in coming to grips with what I was expected to believe and experience concerning the Person and work of the Holy Spirit. I began to encounter those for whom He was not a nebulous being. For such people, He had become readily identified as a vibrant living reality within their lives, a person to know and love and not some vague generic force.

HOW CAN I BE SURE?

More than any other country in the world, we have boundless resources to help us advance in the Christian life: conferences, books, tapes, workshops, services, all designed to impart information. But so often we fail to learn because we are bogged down with doubts, guilt, and fears. The constant cry is "How can I be sure?" As Martin Luther would have crisply informed us, "The art of doubting is easy, for it is an ability that is born in us." It is only the Holy Spirit who can take us through our own doubts and fears and move us into the certainty of what God has for us in Jesus. The Holy Spirit is the only one who is fully aware of all that Jesus really wants to say to us. So Paul affirms, "We speak, not in words taught us by human wisdom but in words taught by the Spirit..." (1 Cor. 2:13). Not only does the Holy Spirit equip God's servants to teach, but He also enables us to learn.

We must never lose sight of the fact that the Spirit has been given in order to lead us into all truth. While acknowledging this, we must always be careful to avoid joining the ranks of those who fail to recognize that truth is here to be lived out and not just to be believed. We must, therefore, be certain that we never sacrifice truth on the altar of our own limited spiritual experience and that we are never content with knowledge of the truth at the expense of experiencing that truth for ourselves.

Simply being prepared to doubt that something cannot be true only because I have never experienced it for myself must be incorrect. It would be equally facile and wrong to suggest that it is sufficient to believe something academically, while never being open to enter into the good of that truth for myself. We must learn to live the truth and be prepared not to compromise it for the sake of our own convenience or comfort zones.

For the Holy Spirit is not content with just feeding our minds. He wants to change the way we feel as well as the way we think. Again it is the Holy Spirit who comes with a divine answer: "I ask God from the wealth of his glory to give you power through his Spirit to be strong in your inner selves" (Eph. 3:16, GNT). Not content with supplying the answers, the Holy Spirit actually brings us the faith to believe them. But that leads us to another question, "Do we trust the Spirit?"

The Holy Spirit works in us and through us, enabling us to live in the way that Jesus always intended. So, then, we do not live God's life through human energies or motivated by our own good intentions. Instead, the power of God is at work in all of us who believe. Now this all sounded great, but I longed to see some evidence for this principle working in my own life. I realized that the promise of Jesus had been that His Spirit would come and not as a mere substitute or replacement. He assured His disciples that even better than the Son of God walking alongside them would be the Spirit of God living *within* them.

Now, "I tell you the truth: It is for your good that I am going away. Unless I go away, the Counselor will not come to you: but if I go, I will send him to you" (John 16:7).

Despite the doubts and fears it was not impossible to believe, but experiencing the joy and release that comes from knowing the promised One intimately and personally—now that proved for me to be another matter entirely! I knew that I was not the only one either, but still that did not stop me from longing for my life to change from just being natural. I longed for a supernatural component to be added, too!

THOUGHT FOR THE DAY

I pray that out of his glorious riches he may strengthen you with power through his Spirit in your inner being.

—EPHESIANS 3:16

WAIT A MINUTE

Uncertainty arrives daily for some, frequently for several, and occasionally for others. Rooted in our own sense of inferiority and insecurity, our uncertainties can often lead to doubts. Many of us know what it is to wake up and find ourselves doubting whether what we said or did yesterday had an impact on anybody. Sometimes we wonder whether the faith we profess is a waste of time and whether we really have honored God by allowing His Spirit to truly work in us.

Now, the fact is that we are only human. If we never doubted anything, we would be some kind of "spiritual superstars." Doubt can be really destructive and undermine our belief in God, but frustration at the level of our experience of God can help to lead us deeper with Him.

Thankfully, God's Spirit lives within us to deal with the problem. He has the answers. The Spirit can, and will, strengthen us with His power deep within to hold on to the faith that we have received and accepted. But then the Holy Spirit longs to fill every fiber of our beings with the love and glory of God. He is also a perfect gentleman and waits for our permission to do so.

QUESTIONS TO CONTEMPLATE

1. How often do you find yourself wondering if there should, and could, be more to your spiritual life?

2. How far do your doubts and fears impede you from moving on?

SPACE TO REFLECT

Let the Spirit of God fill every part of your being, and ask Him to strengthen you when you find yourself doubting. Ask Him to reveal answers at the right time and give you the faith to believe in them.

A TIME TO PRAY

Lord, may I not rely on myself and trust in my own abilities to serve You. Please give me the faith to daily trust You more. Help me to seek to live in the good of Your promise. When I am tempted to be satisfied with my relationship with You and doubt both my worth and the possibility of going deeper with You, I want Your Spirit to work more in and through me, despite my doubt, to bring glory to Your name. Amen.

THE TRANSFORMATION:
THE SPIRIT OF GOD IS AT WORK

SOME YEARS AGO, an American airliner, crammed full of passengers, crashed into the muddy waters of the Potomac River. When I later lived in Baltimore, the location was pointed out to me on several occasions.

Amid all the frantic rescue attempts, a helicopter arrived on the scene, trailing a rope with a safety belt attached. When the men in the helicopter saw an elderly man desperately clinging to some floating wreckage, the rope was lowered, but the man rejected it. Instead of using the safety belt himself, he chose to attach it to someone else.

Feverishly the men in the helicopter winched up the survivor and let down the line to the drowning man. Yet again he saw another needing help and gave him the safety belt. A third time the safety belt was lowered—but the elderly man was gone, leaving only the wreckage floating on the surface.

This is not a bad analogy for the way in which, about two thousand years ago, the Son of God voluntarily relinquished His life in order to serve others. By this means He gave paradise to a dying thief, forgiveness to Peter, and His Spirit to His friends.

DANGER—LIVES ARE BEING CHANGED

The Holy Spirit has always been at work bringing the life of God to us. In Creation, He brought life to humankind. At Bethlehem, He brought the Christ child to be God with us. In an upper room at Pentecost, He brought the power of God to us. Today He brings the life of God within us and constantly empowers us to live out the lifestyle of God. In other words, He is always bringing God to us.

In many ways it was even the same for Jesus. It was in order that He might come down from heaven to this planet that Jesus was conceived by the Holy Spirit and was born in the most down-to-earth way imaginable. But these actions were all done so that He might perform the will of the Father and introduce personal salvation to the human race (Luke 1:32–35).

Then, immediately following His own baptism, Jesus was anointed by the Holy Spirit and, at the same time, the Father spoke to the observers of the scene from heaven (Matt. 3:16–17). There could be few such amazing demonstrations of the powerful work of a united Trinity in action.

It is not surprising that still today we illustrate the corporate work of the Trinity in water baptism—in the name of the Father, Son, and Holy Spirit. This was in exact compliance to the express instructions and wishes of Jesus Himself (Matt. 28:18–19).

But, we may object, how can the living God be satisfied with us as we are? The plain and simple answer is that He is not, so His Spirit works constantly, and consistently, to transform us. He wants to make us more like Jesus.

The Holy Spirit is not satisfied with "business as usual." He is not prepared to leave the new believer with a life that is basically the same as before but with Bible reading, churchgoing, and praying loosely attached to the old lifestyle.

That is why John the Baptist spoke of Jesus as the coming One who would baptize His followers with the Holy Spirit, but also with fire (Matt. 3:11). So the Holy Spirit descended on the 120 who had gathered together on the Day of Pentecost via tongues of fire. These flames were more than a symbol. They indicated the way in which the Spirit comes to burn up the dross and consume the garbage that we have tolerated in our lives. Then He sets us on fire to burn with a new radiance and power. By this means Jesus would separate the wheat from the chaff and would obtain a people who truly loved and served Him (Matt. 3:12).

This power of the Spirit to burn up the old and set us on fire to live a new life is available to all God's people. He longs for us to claim it fully and live in it daily. It may be far removed from the glitzy and glamorous way that the Spirit-filled life has been depicted in many shallow expressions of His coming to provide all that we might require from Him. He does not come to obey our desires but to conform our lives to His purposes for us, and then to keep the Spirit's fire burning within us!

It is at the moment when we realize our inability to do the will of God that we surrender to the Holy Spirit. He then fills us with a divine power that no one on earth could duplicate. The Lord's desire is that we continue being filled (Eph. 5:18) and that we never try to live in our own strength or in past memories or experiences.

The Almighty God that we serve wants to begin with us. If we really are to see an amazing move of God in our nation, then we need to discover the amazing power of the Spirit afresh. Some of us will be called to humble ourselves and pray; others will need to seek ministry and help. But the Lord's heart is that each and every one of us is constantly being renewed by the power of the Holy Spirit.

The result will be seen in a radically transformed lifestyle.

THOUGHT FOR THE DAY

Do not put out the Spirit's fire.

—1 THESSALONIANS 5:19

WAIT A MINUTE

The Lord wants us to be equipped to go out as the early disciples did after Pentecost and leave a mark on the course of history. This may not necessarily mean that we will, or will not, all go out and immediately speak in tongues. But it does mean that our lives will be set on fire, and we will do nothing without the filling and anointing of the Holy Spirit.

QUESTIONS TO CONTEMPLATE

1. Would you say the desire of your heart is to turn this world upside down with the love of Jesus? Why or why not?

2. Do you want to burn for Him?

3. Why do you think you need to have a personal Pentecost experience?

SPACE TO REFLECT

Open your heart to the Lord, and let the Spirit fill you and equip you. Never be afraid to ask, for He has promised to supply the desires of our hearts when we ask in accordance with His perfect will for our lives. Keep on being greedy for more of Him!

A TIME TO PRAY

Almighty God of all power, grace, and authority, help me leave a mark on the course of history. By Your Spirit equip me, with my fellow believers, to go out as the early believers did. Let those around me see Jesus in my life, and let it impact their lives forever. Amen.

Day 24

THE WITNESS:
Truth on Display

JESUS COMMISSIONED HIS disciples to go and be His witnesses: "I have been given all authority in heaven and on earth. Go, then, to all peoples everywhere" (Matt. 28:18-19, GNT). The reason that they could now go lay solely in the fact that Jesus possessed the authority both to send and to equip them. The command to "Go" came directly from the Son, but the supernatural enabling to make a difference in this world would come from the Holy Spirit.

The plain and simple truth is that the lives of ordinary people have never been permanently transformed by the ingenuity of human initiatives or man-made processes, but always by the power of the Holy Spirit. Divine intervention is absolutely necessary for the salvation of men and women. Without the gift of the Holy Spirit, the fantastic early spread of the gospel could never have happened. He was to play a vital role.

Jesus refused to permit His disciples to set foot outside of the city limits of Jerusalem until first He had given them, in His Spirit, all the resources that they would need if they were to fulfill the great task that Jesus had entrusted into their hands. He instructed that they would be "witnesses for me" (Acts 1:8). But first they had to wait patiently for His power. This lesson was to be an important one because the work of God cannot, and must not, ever be attempted only in the strength of man.

When the Holy Spirit took charge, He immediately then produced three distinctive characteristics in the lives of the early believers. He was at work in them to:

☞ Promote compassionate actions (Acts 6:1–3)
☞ Demonstrate spiritual power (Acts 6:8)
☞ Generate bold proclamation (Acts 7:52)

It would be true to say that the Holy Spirit became the energizer of the early church in its goal of communicating the love of Jesus Christ, first to Jerusalem, and subsequently to the ends of the known world. He provided the spontaneous direction as to "where and when" the good news should be shared. Then He generated the outstanding desire to share the faith through public preaching, demonstrative lifestyles, and personal witness. He also took advantage of the everyday life situations of ordinary Christians in order to promote further opportunities for effective witnessing. In that way their outreach was not a learned method or process; it was something that came naturally as each discovered that they were incapable of stopping themselves from "gossiping the gospel" and sharing the truth they had found in the power of the Holy Spirit (1 Pet. 1:12).

When faced with hostility, opposition, and even persecution, they found that they were not alone. They still found themselves compelled to continue to proclaim the truth of Jesus Christ and who He really is. One great example was the apostle Paul. Despite many hazards to health and safety, he never stopped declaring the good news of Jesus Christ to all who would grant him a hearing. He always announced that his motivation was the loving compulsion that the Holy Spirit had poured into his heart (Rom. 5:5; 1 Cor. 9:16; 2 Cor. 5:14).

It is a simple fact that without the Spirit of God, we could not provide an authentic demonstration of the love of Jesus in our world. Scripture is emphatic in pointing out that we are not expected to witness in our own strength but only in the power and authority of the Holy Spirit. He still provides the only effective means by which we can be used to change individual lives and see our world transformed for the Lord Jesus.

DYNAMITE WORDS!

Jesus had promised that His followers would never be left speechless. He promised that "when they bring you to be tried in the synagogues or before governors or rulers, do not be worried about how you will defend yourself or what you will say…the Holy Spirit will teach you at that time what you should say" (Luke 12:11–12, GNT).

Despite that reassurance, many of us are still reluctant to allow God the opportunity to speak through us. We doubt our ability, and we query our intelligence or understanding. Moses had similar fears, but God's reply was straight down the line. Moses said, "I am a poor speaker, slow and hesitant." The Lord quickly pointed out, "Who gives man his mouth?" (Exod. 4:10–11).

The 120 who were in the upper room at Pentecost followed the instructions that they had been given. They waited for the Spirit to come. The Greek word that is used for the "power" of the Spirit is *dunamis,* and that both looks and sounds like our contemporary term for the powerful explosive known as "dynamite." The connection is not inappropriate.

For once they had been filled with the power of the Holy Spirit, then they could move out from Jerusalem and go to Samaria and outlying districts. But it had not stopped there. For they were now exploring what it meant to reach out to the far corners of the globe or "the uttermost parts of the earth" (Acts 1:8).

It is hard to measure the enormous impact (both positive and negative) that these ordinary people made upon their contemporaries, but soon in the wider Gentile world the followers of Jesus were being accused of having "turned the world upside down" (Acts 17:6).

Many of us may long to be like them! Nowadays many very ordinary Christians (if that is not a contradiction in terms) have started to make a new lifetime's ambition. Every day they want to talk to someone about Jesus. They may not feel able or particularly gifted, but they are prepared to trust the Holy Spirit to use them and to offer their mouth for Him to use.

Back in Britain I was always amused at the way one old friend, an Anglican bishop, would confess that he would occasionally become bored on a train journey. To alleviate the boredom, he would walk into the adjacent compartment and ask "Can anyone tell me who Jesus Christ really is?" People looked up, startled and embarrassed, or tried to hide behind their newspapers. Then he would sit down in order to begin to explain more fully!

Not all of us would be able to repeat his performance! I know that I so often fail to share my faith. But we are not alone in having to face this challenge. It is no less than the Holy Spirit coming into our lives in order to enable us to become bolder in our faith.

Now we are not responsible for what happens at the conclusion of our witness; that also is the responsibility of the Holy Spirit. Nor are we judged by results, so none of us are going to receive commissions on conversions. For we each will act as perhaps only one link in a chain. One person may have to face initial antagonism. Perhaps another will confront specific questions, someone else may be used to begin to stimulate interest, and another will explain the way of salvation, all before somebody (or nobody) finally has the joy of leading the person to Jesus.

Yet each was a witness. Each one acted as a link in a glorious spiritual daisy chain, which the Holy Spirit Himself threaded together. For this Spirit is not portrayed in Scripture as one who comes to provide us with spiritual experiences designed solely for our own blessing and edification. Rather He comes to enable and empower us to meet the needs of others. He is, first and foremost, a missionary spirit, given to us so that we might fulfill the work and will of God in our lives by bringing others to Jesus. He is given that we all might become witnesses to the truth we have found in Jesus.

Thought for the Day

You will receive power when the Holy Spirit comes on you; and you will be my witnesses in Jerusalem, and in all Judea and Samaria, and to the ends of the earth.

—Acts 1:8

Wait a Minute

Think of how many lives would be changed if all God's people witnessed with the power of the Spirit, leaving traces of the kingdom in their wake. In the same way the disciples were not sent out in their own strength, but they were sent with the authority and power of the Holy Spirit. So they left traces of His activity behind them.

If they had attempted to witness without the Spirit, their actions would have amounted to nothing. As they began to witness, the Spirit of God moved through them in amazing ways, and lives were transformed forever.

In the same way, if we attempt to witness without the Spirit, we are only engaging in a mere intellectual exercise, attempting to mentally argue our case in order to convince people into the kingdom. But with the Spirit, the job is no longer ours. When it is the power of God working through us, then He does the convincing in order that a life might be permanently transformed.

Questions to Contemplate

1. Do you ever feel that, despite all your good intentions, you sometimes end up witnessing in your own strength, simply using your own natural abilities?

2. How might you become a more effective witness, leaving a powerful trace of the Spirit of God in your wake?

Space to Reflect

We all need to take what Scripture calls a "selah"; it really means "a brief intermission." In other words, we need to pause and seek afresh the power of God's Spirit to equip us to witness in power, not to leave people with a lasting memory of us, but with a lingering trace of the fragrance of Jesus. Such a witness comes only from His own Spirit.

A Time to Pray

Lord, so often I feel weak and helpless in my witness for You. I pray that You will equip me with Your Holy Spirit, that I might witness in power and make a long-lasting, life-changing difference in people's lives for the sake of Jesus Christ's name. Amen.

THE ACTIONS:
They Speak Louder Than Words

Over several years I have had the privilege of watching the living proof of the old adage that actions speak louder than words. And there has been a clearly supernatural dimension to this as time and again I have been allowed to see the Holy Spirit at work in vivid and dramatic ways among the people of God. This has not only been true in Europe or North America, but surprisingly enough it has been most obvious and transparent in the lives of the poorest of the poor and those who live and work among them.

Silviane lives in Haiti. When she was only sixteen years old, the man for whom she worked as a domestic servant raped her. She left the house, but two or three months later found out, to her horror, that she was pregnant as a result of the rape.

Now with a child to look after, she found that the only way to survive was by prostitution. She would sell her body for ten Haitian Gourdes, which is around two dollars. The inevitable result was more children and from unknown fathers. She found it necessary to work the streets all day long in order to feed her little family.

After six years of having to live in this fashion, she found herself occupying a little shack in a vast slum, which served as "home" for several thousand of Haiti's poorest people. This notorious area was adjacent to the headquarters of the Lemuel project, an indigenous evangelical organization set up to offer care and support for those living in such squalid conditions. The director of the project, a warm and approachable Haitian man named Manis, has a simple rule for the staff that is involved in its activities. He insists that there is to be no verbal attempt at direct evangelism until people are first asking questions for themselves. His conviction is that Christian lives should provoke questions, not from what we avoid but what we actually do.

So evangelism in this community has its starting point in the interest created from what the people have witnessed in the compassionate concern and active care for others, which typifies the lives of these Christians.

The only exception he feels obligated to make to this rule are those suffering from AIDS or the chronically sick. Those who may not have enough time left are told of Jesus immediately.

Gigi Munchmore, an American nurse who lived in Haiti for thirty-seven years, met and then befriended Silviane. After several months, she was eventually asked the bitter and honest question, "What are you trying to get from me?" The answer came back that instead of trying to exploit Silviane, Gigi was trying to give her something, and she led her to commit her life to Jesus.

Today, Silviane's home is still the tiny and primitive hut in the vast shanty town situated close to the heart of the capital city of Port-au-Prince. She shares this single room with her five children. Because Silviane is given to hospitality and is reluctant to see people homeless, at times she has as many as eight people living in that one room. That one room is the sum total of the entire dwelling. Loosely speaking, it is "constructed" from discarded pieces of used plywood or tin.

You can only imagine her delight on the day that Silviane discovered her pride and joy, a freshly discarded newer section of a sheet of tin with no holes in it. Joining in the weekly small-group fellowship meeting, she wanted everyone to share her joy and thank the Lord with her. The reason for her excitement is that she now has a small corner of her room where she can sit and not get wet when it rains.

PLEASE BE CAREFUL—GOD IS AT WORK!

Many of us would want to ask what is it that could possibly have made such a difference in the lives of these three people. How can Silviane be so happy at receiving so little? How can Gigi be content to find her mission field in one of the worst slums on earth? How can Manis expect the message of Jesus to be expressed without words? How can Christians find the joy of Jesus when living in such appalling conditions?

The answer can only lie in a supernatural power, in God Himself. To put it plainly, the Holy Spirit has done this.

The kind of Christian life that is introduced by the Holy Spirit is one in which He does the work and we just provide the cooperation. Instead of being satisfied with producing a recital of aspirations that we are supposed to live up to or a list of commands that we are compelled to attempt to obey, the Christian confirms that God has Himself supplied us with the means to live up to His own demands. He has given us His Holy Spirit. (See Romans 5–8.)

It is supremely from lives that have been touched by the beauty of the Holy Spirit that God can speak volumes. Witnessing for Jesus is more a matter of lifestyle than anything else. Our words should never have to be more than an explanation of our lives.

It is through the power and intervention of the Holy Spirit that we can begin to resemble Jesus. We cannot change ourselves into signposts that point away from ourselves and draw other people to Him. It is only the Holy Spirit who can release us from all that we have been and start to mold us into a different likeness. "Where the Spirit of the Lord is present, there is freedom. All of us, then, reflect the glory of the Lord with uncovered faces; and that same glory, coming from the Lord, who is the Spirit, transforms us into his likeness in an ever greater degree of glory" (2 Cor. 3:17–18, GNT).

The Spirit wants to place within our lives the love and compassion of Jesus. He wants us to be people who will always have an open ear to hear and a heart to love those who need help. He wants us to weep for unsaved loved ones and neighbors and be involved in the needs and work of the community so that bridges may be built for Jesus.

If we try to preach the gospel but do not demonstrate the Father's love through our actions, then our words are empty and futile. If we take part in living the life of Jesus and demonstrate His compassion in various ways but neglect to share the reason "why" we are doing it, then we might as well be like any other charity. I have often observed that the proclamation of the gospel without the overt demonstration of social responsibility so often reduces our message to the level of words without deeds. Conversely, our involvement with physical or social need, but minus the good news of saving faith in Jesus, can be interpreted as little more than secular humanism.

When we have willingly acknowledged His authority over our lives, He uses us as living demonstrations of the love of Jesus and the power of His Spirit. In a very real sense we then become the hands and feet of Jesus in this world.

So it is that we can emerge from the shadows of fearful Christian witness into a free, bold expression of the life of Jesus simply because it is His Spirit who empowers us to perform acts and deeds of love that would be impossible in our own strength alone. Some of us will major on words, some on acts of mercy, some on prayer, some on lifestyle, but through each one the Holy Spirit will be actively working out His divine purposes.

THOUGHT FOR THE DAY

Then Peter said, "Silver or gold I do not have, but what I have I give you. In the name of Jesus Christ of Nazareth, walk." Taking him by the right hand, he helped him up, and instantly the man's feet and ankles became strong.

—ACTS 3:6–7

WAIT A MINUTE

In the Sermon on the Mount, Jesus taught the significance of sharing the gospel and demonstrating the love of God in action. He not only taught this as a way of life, but He also lived it.

He then sent His Spirit so that we could follow His example—preaching the kingdom, healing the sick, lifting up the lowly, and so on (Luke 9:2). Jesus did not separate the two. It was always clear that there was a reason behind His loving acts toward people. The Holy Spirit has equipped us not only to love people through our actions but also to give them a chance to respond to the good news of Jesus Christ.

QUESTIONS TO CONTEMPLATE

1. Are you involved in social action or sharing your faith or both? Are the two intertwined?

2. Peter was able to heal the man and share the reason why. How can you do more of the two together in your life?

SPACE TO REFLECT

Consider the importance of actions *and* words as you witness in the power of the Spirit.

A TIME TO PRAY

Father, my heart is to serve You in a way that will bring the most praise and glory to Your name. Help me to know how to serve You effectively, making the best possible use of the time that I have left here on earth. Amen.

Week 4

THE MIRACLES:
EVIDENCE THAT DEMANDS A VERDICT

THE STORY IS told of a pastor in a Muslim nation who lost his life because of his faith. His little church of around a dozen people mourned the tragic loss of their friend and pastor but was comforted by the belief that his untimely death would bear fruit for Jesus in that town. They were sure, along with the second-century church apologist Tertullian, that the blood of the martyrs would always prove to be the seed of the church. The one surprising thing was that nothing seemed to happen.

Ten years later a wealthy businesswoman in that particular city was struggling with some dreadful news that she had received. Her two sons who had left the country and were now living abroad had become Christians! This was appalling news for her, and she redoubled her Islamic prayers for them. But as she bowed her forehead one day to touch her prayer mat, she saw beneath her gaze a small wooden cross. Her sons had not returned to the country, and no Christian had ever darkened the door of her home. It was simply a miracle, and she accepted it as such. She still has that cross, because it brought her to Jesus.

Now this particular lady is a natural-born evangelist, and she just could not stop telling people about this Jesus she had found for herself. Today the little church numbers more than forty people, and it is still growing.

I can only guess that this pastor can now, like his Lord Jesus, look down on the fruit of the travail of his soul and be satisfied. We may well suffer for Jesus, but ultimately His Spirit will work in a supernatural dimension of activity that defies our human imagination.

SPEAKING OF THE GOD WHO WORKS WONDERS

A friend of mine speaks of the way that God is, and has always been, at work through His Holy Spirit. He says that the Spirit, drawing on the example of Jesus, operates through a trio of "words, works, and wonders."

Our verbal proclamation of the good news of Jesus is important, and so is the way in which we demonstrate His love through our actions, but He then can make His own supernatural contribution.

Most Americans regard Iran to be one of the most hostile nations on earth. We view it as a place of tyranny and injustice. My impression from my visits there is that this is not always true. We may dislike the idea of being forced to admit it, but Iran does have a stable government and a developing society. It also has a limited measure of religious freedom.

We never seem to pause to imagine that the church might actually be alive and well and living in Iran! Nor perhaps what it might cost our brothers and sisters in terms of pressure and suffering to live there as Christians and how wonderful the results might be.

While there are still remnants remaining of the ancient Armenian and Assyrian churches that have certainly withstood the test of time, what is still more exciting to me is the fact that new small pockets of believers are emerging in Iran. There are probably more than ten thousand evangelical believers who meet together in around twenty-five small churches. These churches generally find it necessary to meet together in private in order to avoid inflaming public opinion against them or inviting the unwelcome interest of the secret police.

The largest of these would be the Assemblies of God church in Teheran, which has over seven hundred people attending on a Sunday. This particular church is so bold that it advertises its presence by means of a large metal cross that is attached to the front of the building. It is even raised up in the air so that no one can miss it. Recently, the church leaders were interrogated in police custody for the weekend. CNN featured pictures of this church, but few of the viewers would have recognized the powerful, fearless witness represented by the building itself or the believers who regularly worship each Friday within it.

One Sunday an eighty-six-year-old man was tapping his way with his walking stick past the gates of the church. He paused to stop and ask some of those who were standing there whether or not this was the church. They attempted to redirect him to the mosque because they were sure that this must be his intended destination. You can imagine their surprise when he told them that while he had been praying to God for his village, he had seen a mental picture, a vision in which a great white cloud had descended and covered his village. At the very center of the cloud he could see the vivid outline of a wooden cross.

He was quick to explain that this was the reason behind his search for the church. Now that he had discovered that the only way God intended to help his village was through Jesus, he had surrendered his life to this new Savior who he had discovered. This meant that now he wanted to locate the church.

He was asked how far, at eighty-six years of age, he had traveled in order to find the church. His reply was unforgettable. He had journeyed by bus and on foot for more than five hundred miles. Every month from then on he made the same journey in order to break bread with his brothers and sisters in Christ.

Most of the converts in Iran during recent years are people who were once Muslims. But most of them have come to Christ by means of visions and dreams. In other words, when words are not enough, it takes wonders to break through!

I remember there was one church in particular (not in Iran) where I really wanted to preach. God had done a great deal in that church over recent years, and it had become somewhat famous in its locality. So, as you can imagine, I was delighted when the invitation arrived. Perhaps a little more disconcerting was the list of doctrinal commitments that I was not supposed to break. But none of them appeared to be things that I disagreed with, so the requirement did not appear to be particularly onerous. At least that was the case until I arrived at the church and was politely asked if I would "go easy on the miracles!"

It seems to me to be absolutely tragic that in our Western culture we are so fearful of anything that we cannot explain or control. What is more disturbing than that is this is even more so if the miracle comes from God Himself.

We may find it difficult to accept, but in those countries and churches where suffering for Jesus is almost expected, the miraculous intervention of the Holy Spirit in their circumstances has often become a part of their way of life. As in the first-century church, the greater the degree of spiritual fervency and maturity, the more direct the divine intervention.

THOUGHT FOR THE DAY

Now Stephen, a man full of God's grace and power, did great wonders and miraculous signs among the people.

—ACTS 6:8

WAIT A MINUTE

It is amazing to think that our God thought of everything! He knew that the supernatural would serve as remarkable evidence to reveal to mankind that He truly is the way, the truth, and the life (John 14:6). These gifts were never just ordained for the apostles; they were meant for us all.

Miracles can serve as evidence of the power and truth of our Lord and Savior Jesus Christ and are an awesome part of the package we receive! We need always to remember that without the supernatural evidence of the Spirit of God, we would not have had the Resurrection!

QUESTIONS TO CONSIDER

1.   Are you open for God to be God, even when He breaks your rules?

2.   Are miracles for today? If not, then what evidence could take their place in a skeptical world?

SPACE TO REFLECT

Allow the Lord to confirm in our understanding that He is not like a battery running down on power as the years go by. Let us consider the implications of the fact that He is as much alive today in our lives as He was when He worked through Stephen in such power.

A TIME TO PRAY

Father, sometimes I am a bit worried about wonders. I can question or even feel a bit uncomfortable when I hear of what You have done. Yet, at other times I can really get excited. Please may Your Holy Spirit work through my life so that there is always more and more powerful evidence of You in all that I do. Please develop whatever gifts are necessary within my life, so that people around me will become more aware of who You truly are. Amen.

THE LIGHT:
Illuminating a Darkened World

WHEN I WAS a young boy in elementary school in Britain we would open and close each day with a prayer. The one that closed each afternoon began with these words: "Lighten our darkness we beseech Thee, O Lord." It then went on to implore God to keep us safe through the darkness of the night. Now this is all very well, but Scripture itself announced that Jesus brought life to this dying world and that this life could illuminate each and every one of our lives (John 1:3, 9). Instead of always being on the defensive, this light is on the attack and so much so that the darkness cannot understand why it is unable to overcome it (John 1:4).

John the Baptist came to testify to the truth of the light that came in Christ (John 1:7–8). He called on all his hearers to repent, turn around, change their lives, and walk out of the darkness into the light. Many of the early Christians surrendered their lives for Jesus. Brutally mistreated, separated from their families and friends, imprisoned for their faith, they ended up being dipped alive in pitch, placed in enormous candle-holders, and set alight to act as human torches to illuminate Emperor Nero's gardens. Whatever abuse the church suffered, they still provided light in the darkness.

In the same way, we too are challenged to action. We are called upon not to accept the darkness within our society but to work for its change and transformation. Instead of tolerating, accepting, criticizing, or berating the darkness, we are called upon to light a candle with our own lives and actions and dispel it.

CHANGING SOCIETY

We can preserve our function as lights in two ways. One is to protect us from hiding away in a corner to keep our light from blowing out! Another is to launch out into a dark world, confident that the Holy Spirit will not allow our light to be prematurely extinguished.

In many twentieth-century evangelical churches, the idea of total separation from the wider world was often encouraged. This meant that instead of Christian maturity being measured by the impact an individual's life had on the rest of society, it came to be viewed in terms of the degree in which one would withdraw from direct contact with anything that might potentially pollute. It was as if the church had come to a fearful belief that any contact with darkness would always extinguish the light.

If this was true at a local level, it became even more obvious in relation to international matters. What would appear to be vital issues like global poverty, economic exploitation, or human rights seemed to be regarded as vaguely "unspiritual." These "worldly" areas of concern were regarded as more for the rest of society rather than for the church to become intimately involved. It was almost as if evangelicals felt that they could become contaminated if they moved beyond the safety of their comfort zone.

Some felt that too great an involvement in social issues could result in Christians being diverted from their real task of preaching the gospel. Yet, it was often our very own brothers and sisters around the world who were being condemned by this neglect to become the victims of starvation, persecution, slavery, or injustice.

One could gain the impression that many evangelicals became rather proud of the fact that these areas of concern should be consigned to more liberal churches. It may sound harsh, but evangelical Christians only gave the impression of being busy constructing ghettoes from their own church activities where they could feel safe, secure, and unchallenged. For so-called Bible-believing churches the sphere of social, community, and political involvement largely became a "no-go area."

So what did the Holy Spirit come to help us to do? The answer was to lighten our darkness. The last forty years have begun to witness an awakening within evangelical Christianity to the world outside of the church. This has included the verbal proclamation of the good news and both a recognition and involvement with the social implications of the gospel.

Today we recognize that the Lord is concerned with the whole gamut of human life, both physical and spiritual. Organizations as diverse as Focus on the Family, World Relief, Evangelicals for Social Action, The Salvation Army, World Vision, and a whole host of others working either alongside or directly through the local church are helping to transform the evangelical landscape in the United States.

Just as those in the early church cared for the physical needs of each other (Acts 2:44–45; 4:34), so the light of similar loving actions is visible today. A growing conviction has emerged that it is not enough to endeavor to simply keep ourselves untainted from the world. Instead we are here to see it transformed.

Christianity was never intended to be a series of negative regulations that must be rigidly obeyed. We were never intended to merely protest when others disagree with us or denounce their failings while ignoring our own. The Christian life is more than a rigid routine that we must slavishly observe or a process that we choose to follow, but it is a dynamic demonstration of life in the Spirit.

Instead we must allow the light of Jesus to shine out from us, so that all those who share life with us on this planet can acknowledge it. Instead of moaning at those with whom we disagree, we will allow our love to be seen in our actions. This new awareness graphically brings to life the significance of the words of Jesus: "You are like light for the whole world...so that they will see the good things you do and praise your Father in heaven" (Matt. 5:14, 16, GNT).

So our responsibility is not to simply survive here in order that one day we may enjoy the privileges of heaven. Once we have discovered the impact of Jesus on us, we have no right to want to keep Him for ourselves. Our God-given task is to go and reveal His love to those who have yet to meet Him. Now this is easy to say, but it is much harder to put into practice.

For as long as we are called upon to act as the agents of Jesus upon earth and prepare for His return, we have a job to do. This is one reason that the Holy Spirit has been given to us to act as our helper. Because of the aid and intervention of the Holy Spirit, the good news about Jesus would be taken to the whole world. Over the centuries of human history many would be brought to Jesus and would step out of darkness into the glorious sunshine of living in the light of the love of God (John 14:17–26; 16:13).

That is our task. We are here to serve as lights in a darkened world. Because of the indwelling Holy Spirit, we can now know the living God in an intimate personal relationship. Our minds have been illumined, but our lives have been illuminated. We do not merely know about Him through words contained in a book. Nor is our experience second hand. That is what is so different. We can now act as lights in a darkened world. We are sent to illuminate the darkness.

THOUGHT FOR THE DAY

Let your light shine before men, that they may see your good deeds and praise your Father in heaven.

—MATTHEW 5:16

WAIT A MINUTE

We face two dangers. There is always a risk in separating ourselves too much from the world hiding in corners because we are afraid or lack confidence to share the good news of Jesus with others. There is also the opposite predicament of allowing the world to permeate our lives, so that we compromise our faith.

We are called to discover middle ground. First, we need to recognize that we cannot do it in our own strength. Second, we need to begin to allow the Holy Spirit to strengthen us when we are afraid or when we are being too influenced by people. Then third, we allow the Spirit to equip us not just to survive the world but also to engage in it, while not compromising our faith.

QUESTIONS TO CONTEMPLATE

1. How many of us find it difficult to live *in* the world without letting its influence get to us too much? If you ask the Spirit for His help, then He will give you what you need to overcome your struggles of being *in* the world but not *of* it.

2. Do you still have nonbelievers as friends? Do you have opportunities to share your faith with them?

SPACE TO REFLECT

Instead of just wanting the Spirit of God to illuminate our darkness, we should ask Him to show us how each of us can "let our light shine before men" in effective ways. Always remember that lighting a candle is the remedy to dispel the darkness! Maybe He wants to bring someone to mind for us to begin praying for and with whom we can share our faith.

A TIME TO PRAY

Lord Jesus, please equip me with the strength of Your Spirit not just to stand firm in my faith, but to venture out to others. Help me not just to avoid compromising Your truth, but to shine Your light in a darkened world so that all may begin to see Your glory. Amen.

Day 28

The Hope for the Future

I STOOD AT the water's edge and watched the river grow broader, so that it now encroached for several miles inland. Everything had all happened so quickly. For over a week the Limpopo River had received a violent overdose of rain from the passing cyclone, and its banks had overflowed. Fields and roads alike lay underwater. The dams all along the river were filled to the brim. But after days and days of rainfall, the cyclone eventually moved on and the rain stopped.

This same cyclone's path took it into South Africa, and so once more it dropped its rainfall into the Limpopo. The results were inevitable. This time the water poured over the dams and raced into Mozambique. Two days later the young herd boys spoke to me of what it had been like for them to flee for their lives in order to escape the raging wall of water.

The only available place of safety was in the trees; all those who escaped drowning climbed up into their branches. The only problem with that was that the snakes had fled to the same refuge. Never before had I seen snakes, rats, and humans sharing the same place of shelter. Now some half a million people were homeless. They perched precariously on the roofs of the few remaining buildings left standing above the waterline or tenaciously clung to the treetops in strange company as they waited for rescue boats.

Then, once safe for the moment, they hurriedly manufactured makeshift dwellings. These were hastily put together from the refuse on the water banks in order to provide them with temporary homes. Medicines were almost impossible to find, and fresh water was scarce. Some emergency food parcels arrived, but, otherwise, the people had to scavenge for whatever they could find.

Hundreds huddled together for safety on high ground and lined the new riverbanks as they gazed into water where once their homes had been. Amid the desolation I stopped to ask one lady named Lydia the potent question, "Where is God in all this?" Lydia's answer has stuck with me because of the honesty of her reply: "I just don't think God is around here anymore."

Lydia's reaction was very understandable, and we may often be

122

tempted to similar despair. Fortunately, in Mozambique at that time, there were many others who did not see things the same way. They actively responded to the need and provoked many "Lydias" to look at the rescue efforts going on around them and the attempts at rebuilding homes and lives. They began to ask the question, "What is the reason for you doing this?"

The response was not about a "what" but a "who" and could be expressed in a single word—*Jesus*.

NOT JUST ABOUT NOW!

I recognize that few of us will have experienced the depth of grief and desperation that was commonplace in Mozambique. Our own problems, while being no less real, pale in comparison. We feel that we can never properly comprehend the overwhelming sense of helplessness that greets someone who is caught in the throes of a major disaster.

But when we are confronted with the major challenges of life, we too can sometimes feel utterly helpless, but that is when the Holy Spirit insists that we stop groveling and urges us to become part of the solution.

It is easy to say that this should not be a problem for Christians, but it is certainly true that we too will sometimes find ourselves asking where God has gone. We may pay lip service to the idea that the Lord has everything under control, and we place our confidence in Him. But when the rubber meets the road, it is sometimes our fear of the future that rules rather than faith in the God who has it all under control.

For not only does He guide us along the long and arduous roads of our journey, but also He does not allow us to look down all the time. He is the guide who guards our present, but He also lifts our heads up to see the future that He has planned for us (Ps. 3:3).

At its heart the Christian faith is not just about today but also tomorrow. Everything does not necessarily work out now, but certainly all will be revealed later. Every question and dilemma return us to the resurrected Jesus and to where He will take us.

After the agony of the cross and the glory of an empty tomb, He came to His disciples in order to be the executor of His own will and give to them what He had promised would one day be theirs. His Spirit was to be their inheritance, and we have already seen His special gift of His peace. However, there was something else that He also would give to them, and that was the promise of eternity. For this world would not be the end.

It is always a little bit daunting when we read the aftereffects of the resurrection. It is a real challenge to us when we look at what the Holy Spirit did in the lives of the early believers. They came up against so much hostility, opposition, and even persecution (consider Stephen in Acts 7:54ff), yet they were still absolutely convinced that death was not the end and that heaven was waiting for them.

The reason is that the hope of the Christian is an eternal one. It is based upon the promise of Jesus Himself who assured His first disciples that they would one day join Him. This did not apply only to those disciples, but also to all those afterwards who would come to believe in Jesus as a result of their faithful witness.

After His death and resurrection, the ultimate destination of Jesus was not to go back to His disciples, but to return once more to His Father in heaven. This should have come as no surprise to His followers because it was only what had been prophesied for centuries. Indeed, it had been put down in writing throughout the Old Testament. As part of their preparation for the future, Jesus had also announced it to them, but still they were surprised when the Spirit came and Jesus left them.

So He finally ascended into heaven in a cloud. His final act here on earth had been to lift His hands in blessing in order to give hope to those He was leaving behind and to bestow His peace upon them. Both Stephen and John could confidently claim that they had seen the risen Lord ascended in the heavens. The simple expectation of each and every believer is that one day we will see Him, too. The difference is that we will not view Jesus in a vision, but that we will see Him face to face.

Where does the Holy Spirit fit in? He comes to us in order to make Jesus Christ real in us—and He is our hope of glory!

We have become so preoccupied with the priorities of life on earth and with the anxieties of today that we neglect to recognize that heaven is not limited to life with Jesus now; it will be life with Jesus for eternity. Heaven is our ultimate travel destination. Earth is only a staging post on the road to eternity (1 Pet. 2:11).

A day is coming when the situation will be gloriously reversed. Isaiah prophesied that the day is coming when "sorrow and sighing will flee away" (Isa. 35:10) and anticipated a new era and a new day. John heard a voice from the throne that said to him, "Now the dwelling of God is with men, and he will live with them. They will be his people, and God himself will be with them and be their God. He will wipe every tear from their eyes. There will be no more death or mourning or crying or pain, for the old order of things has passed away" (Rev. 21:3–4).

That will be the beginning of a whole new day!

THOUGHT FOR THE DAY

And if I go and prepare a place for you, I will come back and take you to be with me.

—JOHN 14:3

WAIT A MINUTE

It is a disturbing fact that, rather than anticipating heaven as our future hope, we would so often prefer to sit in the safety of our homes and churches, praising God on a Sunday and living in the here and now. Again, it is the Spirit who is our Teacher, and He will not let us sit back comfortably. Sometimes we simply need to be compelled not to settle, but to keep pushing forward.

This is a challenge to us because the presence of the Holy Spirit acts as a constant reminder of the fact that this world is not our home and that He is taking us on a journey where the ultimate destination will be heaven with Jesus.

QUESTIONS TO CONSIDER

1. Do you possess the loving hope of heaven from the Holy Spirit?

2. Are you allowing the Holy Spirit to prepare you for heaven? Are you ready?

SPACE TO REFLECT

Ask the Father to increase your motivation to share His truth and your hope in heaven, no matter what circumstances you may find yourself in.

A TIME TO PRAY

Lord, please help me to hope in You, rest in Your love, and rely on Your Spirit to present me finally in heaven. Amen.

WEEK FIVE

GIFTS AND GRACES

If you do not join in with what the Church is doing, you have no share in this Spirit.... For where the Church is, there is the Spirit of God; and where the Spirit of God is, there is the Church and every kind of grace.

—IRENAEUS
AGAINST HERESIES,
3.24.1 (5,000 QUOTATIONS)

In summary the Holy Spirit in us produces fruit for maturity which builds up the community, while the Holy Spirit upon us releases the gifts for ministry which advances the Kingdom.

—WORDS OF GRACE LEAFLET,
"FAQ's HOLY SPIRIT"

We must humble ourselves before the Body of Christ as we use the gifts so that there may be real discernment and love in testing those gifts.

—BILL SUBRITZKY
RECEIVING THE GIFTS OF THE HOLY SPIRIT

THE GIFTS:
Provided by God

Wʜᴇɴ ᴍʏ ᴄʜɪʟᴅʀᴇɴ were young, I would often come home from a trip and bring them presents. Although this was not an attempt to buy their love, it was successful in getting them to notice that I was back. However, sometimes they seemed to be more interested in the present I had brought than in the fact that I had returned.

Actually I did not object too strongly because pretty soon they would realize that a gift meant that the giver was not far away, and they would turn their attention to the recognition that Daddy was home at last. If they had ignored the gifts I'd brought them and just left them unopened, I think I might be offended! They probably feel similarly nowadays, because they have a better understanding of exactly how long it must have taken me to select, let alone discover, the right gifts for them.

The Holy Spirit is a gift from God. Yet, He in turn has many gifts to give us. If any of us were to be guilty of rejecting or ignoring these gifts, then we would not only run the risk of insulting the Holy Spirit but also perhaps being the unwitting cause of damage to both ourselves and others. For most of these gifts are not just designed to benefit us but were also intended to act as the tools for us to help other people. It is also true that when we are using the gifts, which the Holy Spirit has given to us, then we show most clearly the reality of what it means to be part of the church of Jesus Christ. As Paul wrote to the Corinthian church, "Now you are the body of Christ, and each one of you is a part of it" (1 Cor. 12:27).

Just as each part of our body has a role to play, so each one of us has a task in the body of Christ. Just as a missing body part instantly hampers every other part by its absence, so it is with the church. Jesus always took ordinary people through whom His Spirit could specifically express His gifts and love. The early church continued in the same vein.

What was the reason? Because the church is the body of Jesus, it is not open to division. This body cannot be divided into gifted and ungifted sections. We all have a specific role to play within the purposes of God, and all of us who belong to Jesus automatically become a part of His forever body, the church.

WHAT ARE THESE GIFTS?

We must all avoid believing that the Father only gives gifts to some of His children; this is a lie of the enemy. As we will see, there are more than enough gifts to go around, and God has gifted us all. He loves us equally and desires that we might serve Him in power and confidence. The gifts are given to each one of us to make up the body of Christ. We are called to use the gifts from God to serve Him together, so that the beauty of the Lord is evident to all.

Now there are those who would suggest that these gifts lost their value or even died out completely after the Scriptures were completed. If this were true, then it is at least strange that the Scriptures themselves make no mention of the fact. Whether the list is exhaustive or not, these twenty-seven gifts clearly played a basic part in the life, ministry, and spiritual equipment of the local church during the first century of its existence.

1. The gift of discerning of spirits (1 Cor. 12:10, see Luke 8:29)
2. The gift of the word of knowledge (1 Cor. 12:8, see Luke 18:22)
3. The gift of the word of wisdom (1 Cor. 12:8, see Luke 6:9)
4. The gift of tongues (Acts 19:6; 1 Cor. 12:10; 14:13–33)
5. The gift of prophecy (1 Thess. 5:20–21)
6. The gift of interpretation of tongues (1 Cor. 14:13)
7. The gift of healing (1 Cor. 12:9, see Acts 28:1–10)
8. The gift of faith (1 Cor. 12:9, see Acts 3:6)
9. The gift of miracles (1 Cor. 12:10, see Acts 6:8)
10. The gift of service (Rom. 12:7, see 2 Timothy 1:16–18)
11. The gift of teaching (Eph. 4:13–14)
12. The gift of motivation (Rom. 12:8, see Acts 20:18–31)
13. The gift of giving (Rom. 12:8, see Acts 4:32–35)
14. The gift of leadership (Rom. 12:8, see Acts 13:1–3)
15. The gift of mercy (Rom. 12:8, see Luke 5:12–13)
16. The gift of apostle (Eph. 4:11)
17. The gift of hospitality (1 Pet. 4:9)
18. The gift of celibacy (1 Cor. 7:7)
19. The gift of administration (Acts 6:2–3)

20. The gift of exorcism (Acts 16:18)
21. The gift of evangelism (Eph. 4:11; 2 Tim. 4:5)
22. The gift of pastoral guidance (Eph. 4:11)
23. The gift of missionary (Eph. 3:7)
24. The gift of being willing to face martyrdom (1 Cor. 13:3)
25. The gift of helping (1 Cor. 12:28)
26. The gift of intercession (Rom. 8:26–27)
27. The gift of encouragement (Rom. 12:8, see Hebrews 10:24–25)

Each one of us is individual and different in God's sight. So He equips us with different gifts. Each gift is unique in itself, although many can be employed alongside each other in complementary fashion. Gifts can normally be repeated, although martyrdom and celibacy are clearly unique. There is such a variety to choose from, and most of us are not limited to the possession of just one single gift. In fact, I could suggest that if you can only identify one of these gifts in your life, then you may have it in abundance!

The gifts of the Holy Spirit are given by God to enable the members of the body of Christ to function properly; to enable active participation by all members; and are designed to demonstrate within the body of Christ the *beauty* of God.

We cannot buy or earn a gift. Nor should we use it for our own selfish purposes—it is to be used as God directs. Peter was both quick and direct in his response to Simon, "May you and your money go to hell, for thinking that you can buy God's gift with money! You have no part or share in our work, because your heart is not right in God's sight" (Acts 8:20–21, GNT).

Though we are many, we are one body in union with Christ, and we are all joined to each other as different parts of one body. So we are to use our different gifts in accordance with the grace that God has given us.

If our gift is to speak God's message, we should do it according to the faith that we have. If it is to serve, we should serve. If it is to teach, we should teach. If it is to encourage others, we should do so. Whoever shares with others should do it generously; whoever has authority should work hard; whoever shows kindness to others should do it cheerfully (Rom. 12:3–8).

Thought for the Day

Now to each one the manifestation of the Spirit is given for the common good.

—1 Corinthians 12:7

Wait a Minute

The Holy Spirit is God's gift to us as His children. The Spirit, in turn, gives good gifts freely to us, to be used for the Lord's service. He does not want us to reject or ignore these gifts but to receive them freely. The Spirit's desire is for us to recognize the gifts we have been given, to praise Him for them, and to use them to bring glory to the Father.

If we do not gratefully receive them and respond, we are rejecting a loving and gracious present that the Lord has chosen to lavish upon us.

Questions to Contemplate

1. Consider the gift list earlier in this day's reading.

2. Have you expressed your gratitude for the gifts that the Spirit has given to you?

3. What are they? Have you accepted them? Have you been able to put them to good use in your local church?

Space to Reflect

Set aside some time to be alone with the Lord and ask Him to confirm to you that He has given you good gifts and to show you clearly what they are.

A Time to Pray

Father, thank You that You give good gifts to every believer and do not exclude me. Thank You for the gift(s) You have given me. Help me to use (it) them effectively for You. Amen.

THE TRUST:
Gifts Committed to Our Care

LEARNING WHAT IT means "to live in God's world, God's way" and to correctly use those gifts that He has entrusted to us may not always prove to be easy. Living up to all that God has for us will not always involve traveling along a trouble-free road. He is with us, and He is for us, but that does not mean that our journey will be miraculously free of difficulty.

Jesus acknowledged that His will was only to do the will of His Father who had sent Him. He emphasized that doing the will of God is an essential part of membership in His family: "For whoever does the will of my Father in heaven is my brother and sister and mother" (Matt. 12:50). So I often wish that I had that gaze of simple trust that was the hallmark of Jesus when He said, "Yet not as I will, but as you will" (Matt. 26:39).

Specifically that can also be true in our exercise of the gifts that God has given to us. We always have to be prepared to employ what God has provided.

The gifts are there to be received, but they were also always given with the intention that they would be used. God has entrusted them to us in order that they might be employed for the building of His kingdom, not merely for our own fulfillment or entertainment.

For us the privilege of having been given these precious gifts will always carry with them the responsibility of our using them properly in the Lord's service.

Because each Christian has been given, and must be accountable for, one or more gifts, our commitment to God is seen in the manner in which we handle those gifts that have been entrusted to us. Our responsibility must therefore extend to discovering, developing, and using our gifts. Inspired by the Holy Spirit, the apostle Peter clearly instructed his readers that "each one should use whatever gift he has received to serve others, faithfully administering God's grace in its various forms" (1 Pet. 4:10).

Gifts are part of a "three-way giving." God gives them to us, we offer them back to God, and by His Spirit He equips us to make them available to the whole church. This is because the church is a body and, therefore, a living organism. Christ is the head and, through His Spirit, makes each one of us vitally functioning parts!

Gifts are not the same as natural abilities. Everybody possesses these. But when a life is committed to Jesus Christ, natural talents can often become gifts because they are "saved" along with the rest of a personality. A gift is an ability that is given to an individual by God, out of His love and kindness, or grace. The Greek word *charismata,* which we normally apply to "gift," actually means "grace gifts." Within the strict meaning of the word it denotes every Christian as a "charismatic," and that applies whether we like the label or not! A ministry is the prolonged exercise of a gift. A gift is received rather than achieved, and ministry means serving. A ministry is therefore serving the body with the gift that God has given.

Gifts are permanent because God never takes back what He has given. "For God does not change his mind about whom he chooses and blesses" (Rom. 11:29, GNT). Our responsibility lies in the discovery, development, and usage of God's gifts. So Paul encourages the Roman Christians "to use our different gifts in accordance with the grace that God has given us" (Rom. 12:6, GNT). This is because it is God's will and our welfare that are at stake!

Gifts will often overlap. An itinerant preacher could exhibit the gifts of missionary, evangelist, teacher, and prophet on the same weekend in a local church. Many will combine gifts like motivation and administration in the same personality. In a special course at the Fuller School of World Mission, Carl Cronje said:

> Gifts must be distinguished from baseline responsibilities that *all* of us *share equally*; for example, *all* must pray, *all* must give, *all* must believe *but* over and above the prayer that is demanded of all there is the *gift* of intercession; over and above the giving and believing required of all there is a *gift* of giving and a *gift* of faith. *Gifts* then are built on the baseline; they are the areas where we do far more than the minimum requirement. They are the areas where we find ourselves very comfortable in the Lord. They are the things that make us tick, the itch that only subsides when we scratch it with involvement and commitment. We are "in our element" when we are in our gifts!

Gifts are not to be graded. No one gift is more spiritual than another. As Paul concludes, "The eye cannot say to the hand, 'I don't need you!'

And the head cannot say to the feet, 'I don't need you!' On the contrary, those parts of the body that seem to be weaker are indispensable" (1 Cor. 12:21–22). Nor should we be overly concerned about receiving false gifts. It is true that Satan can and does counterfeit God's gifts. But if our lives are totally surrendered to Jesus, then He is the one from whom we receive.

Whatever gifts the Lord has bestowed upon you or me are special. He gave them to us because He wanted to! He knows that they are the best ones to give for each individual, and so we should never compare our gifts with those of anyone else or be competitive for so-called "better" gifts. Each gift has value in the kingdom of God if it is handled wisely. That is why He has entrusted it to you.

Thought for the Day

The eye cannot say to the hand "I don't need you!" And the head cannot say to the feet, "I don't need you!"

—1 Corinthians 12:21

Wait a Minute

Not one of the gifts of the Holy Spirit is more "spiritual" than the other. All of them are important to God. The Lord has given each and every one of His children good gifts, designed to complement one another and subsequently to help us operate as the body of Christ.

Remember the widow in Luke 21:1–4? What she gave to the offering may not have looked like much, but it was all that she had. This meant more to the Lord than the rich putting in greater amounts that didn't even make a dent in their pockets. The Father sees our hearts, and all He asks is that we use what He has given to us to serve Him. Publicly it may not seem significant, but in the eyes of the Lord it is worth so much!

Questions to Contemplate

1. Do you compare your gifts with those of other people?

2. Do you sometimes covet the seemingly more "spiritual" or "special" gifts that some people have? You need to trust God, the Holy Spirit, to supply what He knows you need.

Space to Reflect

Remember your gifts again! Ask the Lord to forgive you for making wrong comparisons and envying the gifts He has chosen to give to others. May He help you to value yours more highly.

A Time to Pray

Lord, please help me not to see the gifts You have entrusted to other people as more "spiritual" than those I have, but make me truly grateful for what You have chosen to freely give to me. Please help me to use these gifts only to serve You. Amen.

Day 31

THE PEDIGREE:
As It Was at the Beginning?

THE CHURCH TRACES its origins back to the Day of Pentecost (Acts 2:1–13). From the very start, the church recognized the Holy Spirit as being divine, but it was always easier for the believers to grapple with the truth of the Father and the Son and continue to be vague as to the pedigree of the Spirit. Many of the writings of the early church illustrate the acceptance of His identity and general ministry without dissension, but there was little written specifically about the Holy Spirit in the context of Him as a specific subject within the Trinity in His own right.

One significant exception to this general rule was the second-century theologian Irenaeus. He offered his own unequivocal testimony to the importance of the Holy Spirit when he pointed out that in "receiving the Holy Spirit, we walk in newness of life, in obedience to God. Without the Spirit of God we cannot be saved."[1]

As time passes, memories fade, and the same was true when it came to the use of those spiritual gifts that the Holy Spirit provided. With the encouragement of the apostles, the supernatural gifts had been exercised in the local church, but the believers became discouraged when they were abused or overemphasized. (See Acts 21:9; Romans 12:6–8; 1 Corinthians 12:28; 14:1–19.)

Some of those "supernatural" gifts, which are outlined in 1 Corinthians 12:8–10, remained largely ignored by many for centuries. We Christians often tend to run from all that we do not understand. In so doing, we can reflect the spirit of the age rather than the Holy Spirit.

FAR FROM EXTINCT!

Patient study serves to reveal that these gifts do not appear to have become extinct or remained out of use.

Just over a hundred years after Christ's death, three major apologists for the Christian faith, a powerful trio of church leaders in Justin Martyr, Irenaeus, and Tertullian, openly described the existence of many spiritual gifts in the second-century church. Justin Martyr affirmed that "it is possible now to see among us women and men who possess gifts of the Spirit of God." In fact Irenaeus, the bishop of Lyons in France, affirmed the existence of prophecy, discerning of spirits, and physical healing when he wrote, "Others have foreknowledge of things to come: they see visions, and utter prophetic expressions. Others still, heal the sick by laying their hands upon them and they are made whole. "

During the next century, in 246, Bishop Cyprian of Carthage in North Africa wrote to his friend Donatus a personal letter in which he spoke of the gifts the Holy Spirit gave him at his baptism. A far more explicit testimony came from a presbyter named Novatian. He wrote in 257 that the Holy Spirit is "He who places prophets in the church, instructs teachers, directs tongues, gives powers and healings, does wonderful works, offers discrimination of spirits, affords powers of government, suggests counsels, and orders and arranges whatever other gifts there are of *charismata*; and thus makes the Lord's church everywhere, and in all, perfected and complete."

A fourth-century popular heresy claimed that the Holy Spirit was only a created being, but the leading theologians of the day (Athanasius and the Cappadocian Fathers) leaped to the Spirit's defense, but without giving emphasis to the supernatural dimension of the work of the Holy Spirit. But Bishop Hilary of Poitiers disputed that there could be doubt over Paul's teaching of spiritual gifts in 1 Corinthians 12, and even the renowned Augustine of Hippo conceded that the gifts of the Holy Spirit could still occasionally be witnessed in fifth-century church life.

Meanwhile, the alleged conversion of the Emperor Constantine in 312 resulted in Christianity being transformed from an oppressed and persecuted faith into the official state religion. The church became proud of her considerable orthodoxy and became the only visible source of security in a world that was falling apart. Charismatic gifts were generally regarded as having been important in the years of the foundation of the church when society was secure but had later been withdrawn when it was feared that they could rock the boat.

The church saw itself as the only stabilizing agency for society at a time when civil government was disintegrating in the face of pagan invasions, so church authority was emphasized at the expense of individual religious expression. The congregational exercise of spiritual gifts was therefore relegated to a place of insignificance in church life, and "ministry" was seen as belonging to leaders alone. The members of their congregations were viewed as having little to offer.

The next thousand years were notable for the distinct lack of emphasis upon supernatural disturbances in church life. The Holy Spirit was defined as God in us, but no specific activities were assigned to Him. There were always groups and individuals who resisted the constrictions imposed by church and state, and they did see scattered revivals take place. But their activities and publications were censored, and consequently we are short on details (except for the judgments of their opponents) about what they actually did.

During this period the churches in the West abandoned speaking in tongues and regarded it as evidence of demon possession, and the healing ministry of the church was almost entirely wiped out. The Eastern "orthodox" church was different. It largely encouraged both introspection and individuality, and even accepted the idea of shared contributions to "body ministry." The result was that all the gifts of the Holy Spirit, with the possible exception of speaking in tongues, were widely used among orthodox believers.

Then dawned the Reformation of the Western church. Many know that most Calvinists (beginning with John Calvin himself) and their successors the Puritans rejected spiritual gifts. The outstanding seventeenth-century Puritan theologian John Owen wrote that, "It is true that those extraordinary effects of his power, which were necessary for laying the foundation of the church, have ceased."

That was confidently spoken, but again, evidence exists to the contrary:

    ☞ It is claimed that Martin Luther possessed all the supernatural spiritual gifts. He certainly urged one friend to follow the biblical example and pray and lay on hands for the healing of a sick person he was ministering to.

    ☞ The Roman Catholic missionary Francis Xavier is recorded as having spoken in languages unknown to him.

    ☞ Spiritual outbreaks of the gifts took place during the occasional revivals that took place down through the years.

    ☞ Thomas Welsh, one of John Wesley's lieutenants, wrote, "This morning the Lord gave me a language I know not of, raising my soul to him in a wondrous manner."

    ☞ Groups of persecuted Huguenot Christians in eighteenth-century France received manifestations of the power of the Holy Spirit.

Day 31

☞Some of the early Quakers and Methodists experienced speaking in tongues.

This takes us up to the nineteenth century when there were several instances of these charismatic gifts being used in countries as diverse as England, Scotland, Russia, and the United States. Then in 1906, in an upper room on Azusa Street in Los Angeles, California, the Holy Spirit descended, people spoke in languages they had never learned, and the modern-day Pentecostal Movement was born.

BREAKING THE MOLD

We love to pattern things so that, neatly packaged, we can clearly see how they fit into our understanding. God, on the other hand, longs to see us break away from all our presuppositions, pride, and prejudices. His purposes cannot be shackled to our understanding of how they should be performed!

If history shows one thing it is that the living God cannot be confined within our prejudices. It does show that spiritual gifts were extinguished, but it certainly does not indicate that all our spiritual heroes of the past spoke in tongues.

What it does indicate is that it is very dangerous to ever assume that we know what God is going to do next! If God is to be God, then He must reign. It is only too easy to sing songs like "Our God Reigns" and then seek to ensure that He conforms to the way we have always operated. We want things to be done in the manner that we find familiar. The unusual—we sense as uncomfortable—is just not what we are accustomed to. Change, whether originating in God or man, is rarely acceptable to us. Some have pointed out that perhaps our reluctance to see the Lord break through our established norms may reveal more of our lack of flexibility and openness to His will and purpose than anything else.

Two hundred years ago John Wesley wrote these words: "It does not appear that these extraordinary gifts of the Holy Ghost were common in the church for more than two or three centuries. We seldom hear of them after that fatal period when the Emperor Constantine called himself a Christian.... From this time they almost totally ceased; very few instances of the kind were found. The cause of this was not 'because there was no more occasion for them.' The real cause was, 'the love of many,' almost of all so-called Christians was 'waxed cold.' This was the real cause why the extraordinary gifts of the Holy Ghost were no longer to be found in the Christian church."

That is precisely what we must avoid today. As an old friend of mine, the poet Steve Turner, once wrote:

History repeats itself.
Has to; no one listens.

THOUGHT FOR THE DAY

God also testified to it [salvation] by signs, wonders and various miracles, and gifts of the Holy Spirit distributed according to his will.

—HEBREWS 2:4

WAIT A MINUTE

Some sincere people might well insist that the gifts are not needed anymore; that Scripture now supersedes spiritual gifts. Others would say that the gifts cause us to focus too much on the Spirit Himself, ourselves, or on our gifts. A third camp would argue that the gifts are not in any way as important as the fruit. There is certainly truth in each argument.

Nowhere in Scripture did Jesus or His immediate followers declare that the Lord had given good gifts to the early church for them to be forgotten centuries later. He intends that we receive them today and use them wisely. Jesus did not just say to the sick, "I love you"; He also said, "Be healed." Yes, He wants us to love and forgive, but He also wants us to actively use the gifts as a demonstration of the Spirit's power in our communities today! He wants us to work together as a body, building one another up—but for that we need to operate the gifts He has given to us. He desires that we leave a powerful supernatural mark on the course of history, not gradually die out because we quenched the work of His Spirit.

QUESTIONS TO CONTEMPLATE

1. What is my view of the gifts?
2. How is that view going to change the way that I live the rest of my life?

SPACE TO REFLECT

It would be good to ask the Lord to confirm in your spirit "why" He has given these gifts to His children, why they have repeatedly emerged throughout the centuries, and "why" they are still relevant today.

A TIME TO PRAY

Lord, help me not to limit You and the gifts that You have freely given us through the years. I invite You to minister in and through me by the power of Your Spirit, enabling me to contribute to leaving a supernatural mark on history for You. Amen.

THE FRUIT:
What Is It?

*H*ow does testimony of a Christian's life penetrate through to unbelievers today? The fruit is a clear demonstration to others of the Spirit's power transforming you into the likeness of Christ. Love, joy, peace, patience, kindness, goodness, and faithfulness do not arrive in separate packages. They are all part of the same character transformation, and it is so comprehensive that even a world that has been blinded to the things of God finds it difficult to miss.

The presence of the Holy Spirit in our lives determines the fact that we are intended to demonstrate each aspect of the Spirit's fruit and in equal measure. This will be recognized in the different ways that the Holy Spirit is seen to be at work in our lives and in our world.

Fruit-Bearing for Beginners

When it comes to the subject of bearing fruit for Jesus in our daily lives, most of us will simply feel like beginners. The good news is that we are not condemned to achieving this on our own. There is a lifestyle that the Spirit of God wants to create among the disciples of Jesus, but it does not come from any one single stereotype to which everyone must conform. We are all still different, but there are common characteristics that emerge from the fruit that He brings into our lives.

We will never be able to produce spiritual fruit by our own good resolutions or self-effort. It is a natural process, as fruit bearing always is. After all, when did you last see an apple tree in the middle of an orchard struggling for breath, writhing in agony, and screaming to produce apples, stems, and cores? Yet, many Christians seem to try to please God by this kind of process!

What does an apple tree require in order to grow and produce fruit? It needs sunlight, roots, and moisture. Then growth becomes a natural process. In the same way, if we are open to the sunlight of God's love, rooted in our relationship with Him through the Bible and prayer, and relaxing in the fullness of His Spirit, then growth and fruit are inevitable.

The problem for so many of us is that we are still trying too hard! We suffer from our vanity, which demands that we must play a significant part in God's divine activities within our lives. Our insecurity shouts that all must follow the same spiritual pathway that we do. Our fears compel us to strive and go on striving. It is in acknowledging our weakness that we can discover the strength of Christ being exercised by His Spirit within us.

When the Holy Spirit is actively at work in our lives, what should begin to emerge is a transformed character. That is why, in Galatians 5:22–23, Paul speaks of one fruit but with nine flavors—love, joy, peace, patience, kindness, goodness, faithfulness, humility, and self-control. They must always lie at the heart of the Christian life.

This fruit of the Spirit is not designed to be split up or compartmentalized; we cannot choose one or two flavors and forget the rest. It comes as a whole. The Spirit's desire is for us to radiate every quality in our lives. Thankfully, we do not have to do it alone. If we surrender to Him, He works to transform us more into the likeness of Christ.

Both the fruit and the gifts of the Spirit are absolutely vital to the life of the believer. Every major passage in the New Testament on the subject of gifts (1 Cor. 12; Rom. 12; Eph. 4; 1 Pet. 4) is accompanied by a passage on fruit. This is because fruit and gifts are never seen as alternatives but coessentials. The effective exercise of spiritual gifts depends upon the fruit of the Spirit. So the Holy Spirit does not just give His people gifts; He also wants to produce fruit in our lives. One without the other is just not part of God's plan for our lives! The Corinthian church tried to use one without the other and became a spiritual disaster area. As C. Peter Wagner says, "Gifts without fruit are like a car tire without air—the ingredients are all there, but they are worthless."

Both are necessary, because the effective exercising of our spiritual gifts depends upon the fruit of the Spirit at work in us. For example, if we do not exercise our gifts faithfully, kindly, and in love, then what is the point of using them at all?

THOUGHT FOR THE DAY

But the fruit of the Spirit is love, joy, peace, patience, kindness, goodness, faithfulness, gentleness and self-control.

—GALATIANS 5:22–23

Wait a Minute

We do not need to strive to make the fruit of the Spirit active in our lives; we must simply allow God to have His way with us.

Apple trees require sunlight, roots, and moisture to grow. The Lord's desire is that we too are like apple trees. He wants us to be open to the sunlight of His love, rooted in relationship with the Lord through the Bible and prayer, and finally relaxing in the fullness of His Spirit in the Christian community. If we do these things and do not strive, then our spiritual growth is inevitable. We will soon begin to display the fruit in our lives, and then the Lord will trust us further with those gifts we will need to demonstrate more of the fruit of His love in our lives.

Questions to Contemplate

1. When you consider the fruit listed above, which aspects do you struggle with the most and why?

2. Since giving your life to the Lord, are you aware of any progress in some of these areas?

Space to Reflect

It could be very useful to consider quietly whether we are trying to produce fruit by self-effort. How do you need to change focus? Let us each bring to mind again the aspects of the fruit that we struggle with most at this moment, asking God to help us to be stronger and to display more of these qualities in our lives.

A Time to Pray

Lord, I would love to see the fruit of Your Spirit actively at work in and through my life, I long to be more like You. Lord, I ask that my gifts and fruit will work together to bring You glory in my service for You. Please deepen and strengthen my relationship with You so that I can be more effective in ministry. Amen.

DAY 33

THE PRACTICE:
GIFTS AND HOW TO USE THEM

FOR TELEVISION VIEWERS in America, it is tempting to assume that any mention of *The Practice* refers to a popular program about a legal firm. Nothing could be further from the truth. In this context, it refers to establishing a "how do you do it" to putting our gifts into action. It is one thing to know about gifts, but it is another matter entirely to discover how to actually begin to put them into practice. We need to ask the question, "What must we do to use them?"

A friend of mine used to sing a song entitled "God Likes Me." These words always provoke a reaction. It seems impossible that with all our failures and weaknesses, God should actually care about us, let alone entrust us with His gifts! Yet, He has done so, and as the servants in the parable of the talents, we too will one day be accountable for how we have used them.

So the first thing is to recognize that if God loves and accepts us, then we also need to accept ourselves and acknowledge that the living God loves us enough to anoint, gift, and use us. Then we need to put to work that which God has entrusted to us.

I don't know if you share with me a basic distrust that I often feel toward easy systems and "for dummies" books. Under normal circumstances, I would never advocate a "how to discover your spiritual gifts" theory. Yet, we desperately need to be practical on this subject, and I would encourage you to examine this system and use it wherever you may find it relevant in your own life.

FIND YOUR GIFT

In his excellent book *Your Spiritual Gifts Can Help Your Church Grow,* the missiologist C. Peter Wagner suggests this line of discovery.

> An open mind and a teachable spirit are essentials. If we feel we know it all or are too proud to be corrected then we will not function optimally. Some practical suggestions in this regard are:
>
> A. *Explore* all the possibilities by learning the Biblical facts about gifts.

B. *Experiment* with as many as you can. Try to find your aptitude this way. This can be done sincerely. Don't be afraid to fail. It is also important to know what gifts we don't have.

C. *Examine* your feelings. Your interests and your aptitudes when merging will give the greatest success. You will feel comfortable in your gift.

D. *Evaluate* your effectiveness. Don't be too proud to admit where you have not had success. Also don't be too "humble" (falsely) so as to deny where God is using you.

E. *Expect* confirmation from your brothers and sisters. We are often the last to see things about ourselves that are obvious to others at a glance. This is true submission—i.e. teamwork, i.e. knowing where our boundaries of effectiveness are by mutual consultation.

F. *Exert* caution with regard to the particular peril of your gift. For most privileges there is a peril and this is especially true of God's gifts.[1]

Those gifts and talents that the Holy Spirit would bring to our lives are not designed to be used in isolation from the gifts and talents of others. We are to complement other Christians whose gifts will be different from our own.

To that end we need to be careful to recognize those gifts that God has—and has not—given to us. We need to know our giftings. Another wrong concept, which is currently held by a number of evangelical Christians, is the idea that God always leads us in those areas where we feel uncomfortable. That is by no means always the case. God often uses us in the areas of strength that we possess. After all, why would He provide us with a gift if He never intended that we would put it to good use?

But He can also bring surprising areas of gifting to us. After all, He made us, so He knows who we are and what we need. It is as we place ourselves unreservedly in God's hands that He will gift us for His service. Our job is not to do God's work for Him or to ask Him to bless our plans, schemes, or inclinations, but to respond obediently to His initiative in our lives to use the gifts He places within us.

After identifying your gifts, the next stage is to learn how to use them most effectively. The best place to start is to delve deep into the Word of God. Read what happened in the lives of the early believers. A very good place to start would be to consider the letters that the apostle Paul wrote to the churches at Rome and Corinth.

Never be afraid to experiment with the gifts in a safe environment in order to help you to work out which ones you do or do not have. Perhaps ask a friend to give you some insight as well. You will begin to know which gift(s) you have because you should feel comfortable with them, even if they are a challenge to exercise.

We are supposed to demonstrate what it means to truly want to love and serve Jesus, not in our own strength but in the power and authority that God gives. When the Spirit of God is alive and at work within us, then we are known to have a spiritual gift (or gifts). These gifts are for the purpose of building one another up, but they can also provide evidence to the nonbeliever of the power of God.

Finally, we must remember one all-important truth. Jesus, as God's greatest gift, did not come down to earth as some vague, ethereal force. The miracle of the incarnation lies in the fact that He came as a real person. It is a lesson that we must not ignore, for we must never give God the use of our talents and fail to give ourselves.

THOUGHT FOR THE DAY

Each one should use whatever gift he has received to serve others, faithfully administering God's grace in its various forms.

—1 PETER 4:10

WAIT A MINUTE

It is always good to replay the guidelines! We need to find time to evaluate how well we are using our gifts. This means being ready to accept when you are doing well. Sometimes it is easy to be falsely humble! Or, you may need to watch out that you do not find yourself adopting the opposite stance— being too proud about your gifts. Also, be wise about how and when you use them. Remember that accountability is vital. Don't assume that God will only use you in areas where you feel uncomfortable; He often uses us in our areas of strength and springs some surprises on us! Be careful not to cling too tightly to your gifts. They are not given to us for our own selfish purposes, but in order that we might give the glory back to God.

QUESTIONS TO CONTEMPLATE

1. Have you found a friend to talk to about your spiritual gifts? How helpful have they been?

2. How well do you think that you are using your spiritual gifts? Are any lying dormant?

SPACE TO REFLECT

Ask the Spirit to effectively equip you to use the gifts He has given you and to highlight when and where you can be most effective in using them.

A TIME TO PRAY

Lord, help us all to use the gifts that You have given to each one of us individually in the best possible way. Help me not to be proud or falsely humble but rather to use them purely to serve You. May my focus always be You and Your Spirit and not me and my abilities. Amen.

DAY 34

GIFTS THAT SOMETIMES
CAUSE A PROBLEM!

So HERE IS the good news! The Lord has given us gifts to use, and we are not to allow them to stagnate or to remain unused. They are always to be strictly operational. However, depending on the kind of Christian fellowship that we enjoy, we need to be aware that some gifts will be more popular than others. These gifts can be placed in three groups:

- Gifts of revelation (the power to know)
  Discerning of spirits, word of knowledge, word of wisdom

- Gifts for activity (the power to do)
  Gifts of healing, the working of miracles, the gift of faith

- Gifts for communication (the power to say)
  The gift of tongues, the gift of interpretation, the gift of prophecy

The truth is that using our spiritual gifts will change our lives but only for the better. Realizing and beginning to exercise the spiritual authority that we have been given can only result in a more fulfilling life as we see God work in and through us in amazing ways. Yes, it will be challenging and hard at times, but life in the Spirit is incomparable with life without Him. So let us examine the gifts that God has given.

THE POWER TO KNOW

Discerning of spirits
This is different from natural judgment; it is simply the mind of Christ being revealed through a believer. This is a very necessary defense, particularly where the gifts are concerned. We need to differentiate between what comes from God, what comes from the opposition, and what is coming from ourselves. Jesus warned His disciples, "Watch out that no one deceives you" (Matt. 24:4).

Word of knowledge
This is the supernatural revelation of information by God that was

150

not learned by the efforts of our natural minds. We see it, for example, when Peter exposed corruption in the church in the case of Ananias and Sapphira (Acts 5:1–11). Often Christians counseling others experience that quiet moment when God reveals in their hearts the real problems that lie beneath those surface issues dominating the conversation. What to do with that information poses a different problem, and God has another answer.

Word of wisdom

This constitutes supernatural revelation as to what action needs to be taken in a given situation, often after the word of knowledge has first been employed in order to expose the exact nature of the problem. This is when we really need to proceed with caution. Sometimes we can even be persuaded that we need to try to give God a helping hand, even if it is for the best possible reasons. What we then say will cease to be His message and inevitably will be reduced to the level of becoming only ours. As we progress in the life of the Spirit, our ability to hear the Lord will develop.

THE POWER TO DO

Gifts of healing

Ninety percent of the recorded ministry of Jesus on earth was devoted to healing the sick. His first instruction to His disciples when He sent them out was to "heal the sick" (Matt. 10:8). After His death and resurrection, He performed no further healings. Immediately after Pentecost, the disciples began to heal the sick, raise the dead, and cast out demons, fulfilling the words of Jesus: "I am telling you the truth: those who believe in me will do what I do—yes, they will do even greater things" (John 14:12, GNT).

The working of miracles

Miracles were a constant feature in the life of Jesus and in the experience of the early church. Prison escapes were arranged (Acts 5:17–25; 12:1–17; 16:25–40). Paul survived the bite of a deadly snake with no side effects (Acts 28:3–6). In recent years miraculous events have been documented all over the world. The purpose of a miracle is to meet human need and, in line with the continuing ministry of the Holy Spirit, to bring glory to Jesus. If it fulfills any other purpose, be careful; Satan can produce all kinds of demonic counterfeit miracles, but they can never glorify Jesus!

The gift of faith

From the moment we are born again, faith is in operation within our lives and our daily experience. When we learn to trust Jesus, we also become open to that faith that the Holy Spirit produces as a fruit in our lives. We do need, however, to distinguish between faith and foolishness. The Holy Spirit will not just do what we demand. He brings glory to Jesus and only acts in accordance with the will of the Father. It is as we ask God to lead us into His way, and confirm it with our brothers and sisters, that we can move out in confidence. What God has told us to do, that He will honor.

THE POWER TO SAY

The gift of tongues

This refers to the ability to praise God in an unknown language that may originate on earth or in heaven. We shall say more about the place of this gift in worship later.

The gift of interpretation

This is the ability to understand what is being said when someone speaks in tongues. Without it, tongues would remain incomprehensible.

The gift of prophecy

The power to speak God's word should produce powerful and direct results. It may operate as a direct revelation or it can be mediated through preaching or prayer. Prophetic praying or preaching can be an important vehicle in God's hand as we surrender our words to His control. Hearing God speak through ordinary people in this way can provide "help, encouragement, and comfort" for Christians (1 Cor. 14:3, GNT), but it can also lead unbelievers to the incredible conclusion that "truly God is here among you!" (1 Cor. 14:25).

The Lord does not want us to be afraid of the gifts that He gives to us. Some of us find ourselves neglecting to use what He has given because of fear. We think that we will not use them adequately, or we believe that we are not "good enough" to use them. Others of us have a fear of operating in our gifts because of how it might change our lives. We prefer a comfortable, safe life to a useful one. There are also some who have witnessed the abuse of these gifts and therefore remain extremely cautious about them.

As we become open to the Lord, He can give us gifts and use us. Our part is to be sure that the glory never comes to the gift or to the recipient of the gift, but only to God Himself. He alone is the giver of every good and perfect gift. Our responsibility is only to use these gifts in a way that will build up one another and extend the ministry of the kingdom of God.

THOUGHT FOR THE DAY

Each one should use whatever gift he has received to serve others… if anyone speaks, he should do it as one speaking the very words of God.

—1 PETER 4:10–11

WAIT A MINUTE

Comfort and safety will never make a difference to the kingdom of God, but stepping out in faith and trusting God to use you could make eternity a very different place.

God gives the gifts to you. You offer them back to God, and by His Spirit He helps you to make them available to the whole church. He gives you the gifts with no intention of taking them back. He just asks that you involve Him in your use of them, so that He can melt away your fear and breathe through you in power.

QUESTIONS TO CONSIDER

1.   Are you afraid of using your gifts? If yes, explain why.

2.   What do you think is holding you back?

3.   What must change to help you use those gifts?

SPACE TO REFLECT

Ask God to help you to put your trust in Him as you step out and try new ways of exercising your gifts.

A TIME TO PRAY

Father, help me not to be afraid of the gifts You would give me or fail to use them for Your glory. May I not misuse or abuse them and act as a stumbling block to others. Amen.

DAY 35

THE NATURAL VS. THE SUPERNATURAL

ONE THEORY CLAIMED that if God had indeed ever existed, He brought this world into being as an elaborate mechanical creation that, once wound up like a giant clock, He abandoned to pursue other activities. In other words, He took a "leave of absence" once we had dramatically "come of age" and were quite capable of coping alone.

If God had effectively locked Himself out of this world, then the possibility of supernatural intervention in the affairs of this world had departed with Him. He was to be replaced by self-reliance. In His absence the inevitable conclusion was that we ourselves must represent the only real hope for the future. Only the present material world was viewed as having reality. There could be no divine, miraculous, or supernatural forces in the universe. Many recognized forces existed that simply defied human explanation, but they simply denied that these could be supernatural in origin.

Such views prevailed throughout the first half of the twentieth century. Then popular support for this perspective began to wane. The problem was that after two world wars, the origination of the atomic bomb, starvation on a worldwide scale, and a raging AIDS epidemic of global proportions, the utopian dream had begun to look like a hollow sham.

The mood of optimism had been replaced by one of pessimism and despair. A new faith was needed to stand in the gap. It is true that there was a growing and genuine hunger for spiritual realities and fulfillment, but instead of a return to Christian truth and the living God, people chose to turn to self-exploration and the old discredited mystical and pagan beliefs.

In this mix the concept of a personal God was seen as being not "trendy" or as being unreal or irrelevant. It became widely accepted that a consistent advance in scientific understanding could meet all the needs of modern society. After all, human reason could quite adequately produce its own answers to the whole gamut of problems that might confront humankind. Technological growth has provided the confirmation for most people that God is no longer necessary for life in a modern world. After all, who needs a healer or a miracle worker when there is a hospital just down the road?

154

In fact, modern man has become the quintessential self-reliant being, or, for the moment, he may think that is the case!

IGNORING THE GIFTS

Two Christians were talking together, and one said to the other, "Well, you can have the gifts. I'll take the fruit." My response to that would be I want to have all that God has to offer. Quite honestly, I need all the help that I can get!

We need to both recognize and value the fruit and gifts alike, because the Holy Spirit working in the life of the believer produces both. Each should be carefully evaluated alongside the teaching of Scripture. We will never begin to understand the significance of gifts and fruit alike until we view them in the proper context of what the Bible teaches us about the Person and the work of the Holy Spirit. For it is who the Holy Spirit is that determines what He does.

If we choose to ignore these gifts, then it will be necessary to face up to the fact that we are running risks in two major areas:

1. By removing the supernatural ingredient from biblical Christianity, we throw an open invitation to Satan to fascinate society by his own subtle, but completely inferior, tricks.

2. We can fall into the trap of reducing Christianity to the status of an alternative philosophy. The emphasis on miracles in Jesus' personal ministry indicates the way in which He provided for our faith to be seen in the context of the supernatural activities of the living God among men and women.

Because these gifts have caused both disagreement and division due to the dangers associated with their abuse, we must look in a little more detail at what the Bible has to say about them. Three primary objections have been given to the use of these gifts today.

"We don't need these gifts."

There is nothing in Scripture that suggests that these gifts are not for the people of Christ in any age. An honest, penitent, and expectant quest for a closer walk with God and a deeper knowledge of Him will always be rooted in an understanding of all that Scripture leads us to anticipate as a part of our birthright. While conclusions will differ, we need to be careful neither to deny nor slavishly follow the verdict of others.

"These gifts focus our attention on the wrong person."

The Holy Spirit does not seek to bring attention to Himself because His function is to bear witness to Jesus. The danger can therefore come in the way that these extraordinary gifts can focus undue attention on either the Holy Spirit or the gift itself, or even upon the person exercising the gift. One safeguard is that these gifts should generally be practiced in the context of a local church or fellowship with all the accompanying safeguards of structured authority. Scriptures give us a further standard to which our practices must conform. Christians should not follow signs; signs should follow Christians.

"The gifts of the Spirit are not as important as the fruit."

The simple fact is that the gifts of the Holy Spirit represent various ways in which the power of God works in and through the life of the believer. The fruit of the Holy Spirit is the character and nature of Jesus Christ being shown in the life of the believer. Therefore, Jesus not only said to the sick who came to Him, "I love you," but He also said, "Be healed!"

Surely one of the saddest things to experience is to know what it means to love someone and yet be incapable of helping him. When we have become conscious of all that God is offering us, then we must always be prepared to accept all that He wants to give us, even if it creates theological problems for us!

THOUGHT FOR THE DAY

You stiff-necked people, with uncircumcised hearts and ears! You are just like your fathers: you always resist the Holy Spirit!

—ACTS 7:51

WAIT A MINUTE

"How could they get it so wrong?" we find ourselves asking when we read a biblical passage such as this. "How could they actually stone Stephen to death because of his claims?" You and I know his claims are the truth, and yet the Sanhedrin dangerously opposed his words.

Scarily, we live in a similar world today. We may not all be stoned for our faith, but we do inhabit a world that believes in itself, over and above a powerful, living God! And a world blinded, just like those who denied that Jesus was the Christ in the early years of the church. Today the issues are different, but the truth stays the same.

The hope is that more people might realize that dependency on mankind is not the answer. In the face of increasing natural disasters, perhaps this time hope and truth might be in the right place.

QUESTIONS TO CONSIDER

1. Why do you think that in today's world, people feel that they can make it on their own?

2. Do you sometimes find yourself believing that you can cope alone? If so, why?

3. Inhabiting a self-reliant Western culture, yet in the face of the recent world disasters, how might you use the power of the Spirit in your life to share the truth of Christ?

SPACE TO REFLECT

Ask the Lord to give you the confidence that Stephen had in the power of the Holy Spirit. Begin to believe that it really can make a difference, even in such a technologically developed part of the world!

TIME TO PRAY

Father, thank You that we are not cut off from You. Thank You, Lord, that we do not go through life having to rely on ourselves. I praise You that I have found hope in You. Please help me to convey that truth in the power that You have given me. Amen.

WEEK SIX

SPIRIT-FILLED CHURCHES

The consequence of a Spirit-filled life is a heart that desires to minister to others, a heart that experiences joy, a heart that is grateful, and a heart that serves.

—MAX ANDERS
*JUST THE FAQ*s ABOUT THE HOLY SPIRIT*

Faith and obedience are bound up in the same bundle; he that obeys God, trusts God and he that trusts God, obeys God. He that is without faith, is without works and he that is without works, is without faith.

—C. H. SPURGEON

Day 36

The Church and the Spirit

SOMETIMES WE BECOME so excited with the fact that the Holy Spirit arrives to make His home within our lives that we forget that He also comes to introduce us to the privilege of becoming a part of a whole new family. In other words, we neglect to recognize that this same Holy Spirit acted as the midwife involved in bringing to birth the church of Jesus Christ.

Not only does the Spirit bring to our lives the joys of personal salvation, but He also introduces us into the realities of becoming part of what He has intended to be a different kind of community, no less than a whole new alternative society.

This is an amazing truth. The Holy Spirit did not come just to deal with us as individuals, but as part of a corporate whole. So His work is not just about "me and Jesus," but He is about "you, me, and Jesus" and the rest of the family as well!

Life-Changing Church!

We were created and prepared to be His church. This is never something that we can achieve separately but only together. The simple fact is that the Christian faith is inescapably corporate. So we know that the Holy Spirit unites us all together through our shared relationship in Jesus. That is why we are now part of the same family. We are brothers and sisters in Jesus Christ. Unlikely as it may seem, we really were made for one another!

It would be true to say that church constitutes a clear demonstration of God's love. He has not left us to struggle through on our own; He has given us a family. This family is not just intended to shore up our defenses and ensure our survival. It lies at the very core of God's action plan. Put simply, the church lies right at the heart of His eternal purposes. It would be true to say that where God intends to act within the world He is going to do so by His Spirit and through His church.

Nowhere has this been more prevalent today than in Albania. Who would have ever predicted that Albania could provide one of the single most outstanding demonstrations of the church in action at the conclusion of the twentieth century?

Situated in the Balkans on the Adriatic coast and adjoining Montenegro, Macedonia, Greece, and Kosovo, Albania was the poorest and least-developed country in Europe. The devastation that was inflicted by more than forty years of communist rule will continue to haunt this small country for many future decades. During four long decades Dictator Hoja had locked up Albania and threw away the key.

The problems afflicting Albania were not only economic. Spiritually, the nation had endured genuine hardship and loss. Thanks in part to the sterling efforts of an American missionary and his colleagues, there was a small cluster of evangelical Christian congregations existing in Albania at the time the Communists came to power. By the time their reign was over, there was only a handful of survivors. From that tiny remnant of only five individuals, God was going to rebuild His church. By 1999, none of the original five remained alive, but there were now around eight thousand evangelical believers in that small nation.

It was at that moment in time that half a million Kosovar Muslim refugees poured across the border. It would have been so easy for the Albanian Christians to reject the Kosovars. They came from the wrong religion, culture, and income bracket. Yet these young churches began to vividly show what it means to put into practice the principles that Jesus announced over two thousand years ago. They demonstrated the reality of Christian love in action.

When the crisis was over and the Serbs had conceded defeat, the Kosovars began the long journey back to their burned-out houses, ruined crops, and destroyed property. This time they did not travel alone. A number of Albanian Christians declared that they were coming along, too. They declared that these were now a part of their family, and today they work together rebuilding homes and helping to reconstruct shattered lives.

This is church, a visible reminder of the fact that the Holy Spirit never intended that we would have to stand alone. Furthermore, it provides a graphic illustration of the way in which the Holy Spirit intends us to recognize that the Christian faith does not consist of just what an individual thinks or believes but has its clear and visible expression in what we do in our daily lives. It has sometimes been said that actions speak louder than words, but it took the Albanian churches to teach me the truth of that statement. Church can only truly be church when the Holy Spirit empowers it to be church in action.

The church is important because it is the heartbeat of Jesus. When we become part of God's family, we do not merely discover a common faith that we can share with Christian colleagues; instead, we actually become brothers and sisters with each other, because now we share the same heavenly Father. In other words, the church is not just the neighborhood church or fellowship where I go to worship God. It is far bigger than that. For the church is not only local; it is universal. It consists of all those around the globe who pledge allegiance to Jesus as their Lord and King.

THOUGHT FOR THE DAY

> I have given them the glory that you gave me, that they may be one as we are one: I in them and you in me. May they be brought to complete unity to let the world know that you sent me and have loved them even as you have loved me.
>
> —JOHN 17:22–23

WAIT A MINUTE

A team of ten was involved in a one-week missions trip. They built relationships with young people in the town and concluded the week with an evangelistic event. Although many gave their lives to Christ at the evening event, the feedback from the young people suggested there had been much more to their decision. Several of them commented that they could not believe the love and care among the missions team. They were astounded that there were no ill feelings in the group and that they were all serving with the same heart and the same deep love for one another. The Spirit's work in the relationships had spoken dramatically to the youth.

With reflection, it seems that this unity among the missions team was just what Jesus desired for His church. We can see the same love among the early believers in Acts, and it drew many to Christ (Acts 2:42–47). To fully reflect the God that we serve, we need to be "one as they are one." The Holy Spirit will minister in power to reveal the Lord's awesome love, if the church conducts itself primarily in love.

QUESTIONS TO CONTEMPLATE

1. Do you feel that there is unity in your church? Why or why not?

2. How might you operate more as a family in Christ?

Space to Reflect

Let this idea sink in: the Spirit of God enables us to have unity with one another within the body of Christ. We do not have to strive to make it happen on our own.

A Time to Pray

Lord God, it is amazing to think that You are One. Thank You that Your church is the vessel through which You want to display that loving oneness. Please help me, as a member of Your body, to encourage family, so that Your love may be seen by those who do not know You. Amen.

DAY 37

THE SERVICE FOR THE KING

THE HOLY SPIRIT always seeks to bring transforming change and renewal into the life of the local church. Sometimes we are guilty of falling into a tempting trap. We view this desire as simply relating to the provision for us of the latest spiritual experience that has been thoughtfully designed for our enjoyment. To relegate the Holy Spirit's activities in the life of the church to this selfish level or to reduce His ministry among the people of God to solely this type of activity is to make a tragic mistake.

It is the task of the Holy Spirit to make the invisible church visible to the gaze of a watching world. For too long we have emphasized what the Spirit is doing for us, but He is not our Spirit. He is not available for our own domestication; we cannot make Him into what we want Him to be. He is no less than the Spirit of Jesus. As such, His task is supremely to focus attention away from the structures of the church, or just the satisfaction of the people attending, and onto the Lord of the church Himself.

So how can the Holy Spirit fulfill this ambition through the local church? If we really are serious in wanting to know the answer to this question, then there is much that we can learn from other churches and from our brothers and sisters around the world. Supremely we must examine what Scripture has to say on the subject. There again we should need not only to review what instruction it gives but also be prepared to learn for ourselves from the models that it provides.

THE VISIBLE CHURCH

It almost goes without saying that we would not go far wrong if we were to follow the model of the Jerusalem church. It certainly represents an effective model of what the church ought to look like. We must surely ask whether this is what the Holy Spirit would want us to resemble, for this local church was less preoccupied with the many personal blessings they received, but they were more concerned with other things such as:

- Freedom from social discrimination

- Demonstrating their concern for each other by sharing meals, housing, and voluntarily surrendering property

☞Spreading the good news of the kingdom

☞Appointing leaders to the administration of social programs

☞Caring for the poor, widows, and orphans

☞Healing the sick

Jesus had preached and demonstrated justice for the poor. It is significant that the early Christians were obedient to Christ's demands. Already the Jerusalem church as a community was putting His principles into practice. It is not therefore surprising to note that a concern for the poor remained a hallmark of the early Christians (Acts 9:36, 10:4; James 1:27–2:4). But God never forgets the generosity of His people. It was all going to come home to them. When famine came, Paul organized emergency relief. Those who had given so generously would now receive (Rom. 15:25–27; Gal. 2:10).

Does this makes you feel as uncomfortable as I do when confronted with this model? Too often we prove to be guilty of confining the operations of the Holy Spirit to the cozy, privatized area of my church, Jesus, and me. Actually, He wants to do something far more radical. He wants to take what He has done in renewing both our individual and church lives and use this as a launching pad to lead His church back to the adventure of both challenging and transforming our world.

God called His people Israel to be unique and to be an example of social concern. They were to be committed to the refugee, the poor, needy, widowed, and orphaned; they were to be ruled by justice, peace, and love, with no slaves or elaborate social hierarchy. For our part, we need to face up to the serious question of whether or not we give to the poor, the elderly, or to the disadvantaged.

It is a sobering question to face honestly, but if the lifestyle of the Jerusalem church represents what the Holy Spirit does in the life of a local church, then how would we rate ourselves? On the basis of the evidence that is provided by our lives within our own community, both individually and corporately, can we be sure that He is alive and well and operating freely out of your church and mine? Or have we stopped short, stuck somewhere between the realities of Calvary and a genuine Pentecost?

THE SPIRIT IN THE WORLD

The Holy Spirit is given to be our helper today, to encourage us to meet those needs that exist on our own doorstep. So the call comes to be distinctive both in what we say and in what we do—speaking God's Word into situations and getting our hands dirty. The call to servanthood, giving, love, and prayer is the message of the Holy Spirit to us today in order that we might be for others "the Word in working clothes."

Above all we were called to make a difference in this world. For this reason the Spirit has come to make us to be salt and light within our society. These are the twin demands that Jesus lays upon all of us (Matt. 6:13–16). He does not give us the right to choose between them, for the two are inextricably intertwined in God's purposes for His people. If, by His grace, we are to change our world, then we are not at liberty to just choose the one that appeals the most to us and ignore the other. Biblically the two come as a combined package, for evangelistic proclamation and social demonstration are not to be divorced from each other.

To have social action without the gospel would accomplish little more than the puny efforts of secular humanism. But taken the other way around, we are too often left with the barren emptiness of words without deeds. In the Sermon on the Mount, Jesus uniquely teaches the significance of both and the strategic importance of their standing together. We must be very careful to never allow our own prejudices, traditions, or preferences to take precedence over the Master's instructions.

As we face the needs of those who suffer from a variety of social ills, the Holy Spirit issues specific calls on our lives. The elderly, unemployed, refugee, sick, disabled, immigrant, low-wage earners, those living in overcrowded living conditions, those in ethnic minority groups, those not yet born, and many others, all need to see the demonstration of the love of Jesus.

Just as the Jerusalem church, living in the power and authority of the Holy Spirit, had proved herself to be a servant of a different kind of kingdom, so it is only when the church is no longer seen as an impersonal, authoritarian institution but a caring and helping body of real people will it truly reflect the character of its servant King. As Jesus Himself had to remind them, "If anyone wants to be first, he must be the very last, and the servant of all" (Mark 9:35).

THOUGHT FOR THE DAY

All the believers were one in heart and mind. No one claimed that any of his possessions was his own, but they shared everything they had.

—ACTS 4:32

WAIT A MINUTE

It is very challenging to examine the life of the early church and to see how powerfully the Spirit of God moved through them. It may be exciting to see how the gospel quickly spread, but when you compare it to parts of the world church today, it is a hard pill to swallow.

If we can begin to move more toward the following two concepts together, then the Spirit will be free to work. First, we need to move away from the idea that the church is the building we go to on a Sunday. The church is a body—you and me, not a building! Together, we are the living embodiment of Christ doing His work. Second, we cannot return to the legalism brought about by Old Testament law. The love of Christ has overridden the law, giving us freedom in the Spirit. It is terrifying if buildings and rules are what people think of when we talk about church, especially when our hearts want them to see a loving body reaching out to help them.

QUESTIONS TO CONTEMPLATE

1. How do you think your non-Christian friends would describe church?

2. If it is negative, how do you think that we, as believers, can change their perception?

SPACE TO REFLECT

Consider the trademarks of the early church (noted in reading), and ask yourself where the weaknesses are in your church.

A TIME TO PRAY

Lord, thank You that You do not give up on Your church. Please help us to allow the Holy Spirit to operate freely within us and through us—showing us how we might make effective change. Amen.

THE WORSHIP:
A NEW DAY DAWNING

LOOKING DOWN FROM the platform I could see a miracle happening among the congregation below. Just row after row of Christians praising God—each one comfortable as they worshiped in the way that came most naturally to them, but all choosing to express their worship in different ways from others around them.

One had his arms straight up in the air, while his neighbor's hands were firmly at her sides. Next to them stood a married couple, the husband with his hands outstretched at hip height, his wife with hers grasping their song sheet. Another man had his hands in his pockets, while his wife danced up the aisle! All were worshiping God in their own way. Some offered their hearts and lives to the Lord in a quiet meditative fashion; others expressed their sense of joy and gratitude with total abandon!

For so long we have been processed into the "right" way of doing things that uniformity has been the order of the day. But on this occasion my eyes strayed along a row to see all the glorious variety of Christians in worship, each accepting the others, differences included!

This variety is important. Each needs to be comfortable in offering to God their own worship, refusing to be thrust into the straightjacket of copying their neighbors. The miracle will take place where no one is dismissing his or her brother or sister as being either too emotional or too traditional. A quiet spirit of mutual appreciation is beginning to release us into allowing one another to be who we are in Jesus.

COMMUNICATING THE CONCEPT OF WORSHIP

Worship is one of the great words of the church. Unfortunately, words can easily be misunderstood, and a word regularly used can prove the old adage that "familiarity breeds contempt." So the more we talk about Sunday morning worship, the easier it is to equate "worship" with our church activities preceding the sermon!

Worship must be an expression back to God of what He is to us! In some appropriate manner, be it singing, prayer, reading of Scripture, meditation, or some other means, we express "a humbling but delightful sense of admiring awe and astonished wonder."[1]

Worship can only happen when we've stopped trying to stand before God and speak our own wisdom. It is for those who are being humbled into a true understanding of themselves as creatures before a Creator. Then comes the giving of time, and silence, and wonder, in admiration and awe before the living God. As Jesus said, "I will show you whom to fear: fear God" (Luke 12:5, GNT).

Worship incorporates the praise of a grateful people, joyfully acknowledging all God has given us.

So God is enthroned on the praises of His people. But how?

1. **In corporate worship:** not just going through the motions of a well-established routine, but bringing a specific offering from our own hearts to the Lord. Whether it is a prayer, a song, a reading, a hymn, or a word from the Lord, we all bring our contribution.

2. **In meditation:** In our frenetically busy world it can be incredibly therapeutic to simply take time—on the bus, at the kitchen sink, during lunch—and allow just a phrase of Scripture to start to minister the truth of God's Word to us. Digest it, and worship Him!

3. **In praise and prayer:** The worship of a grateful heart is expressed in thanksgiving to God for all that He has given to us. There has been a rediscovery of the biblical understanding that our bodies can be used in worship. Dance, either in specially choreographed sequences or as spontaneous expression of praise to God, has opened new dimensions for some, while others have found that the lifting of hands to the Lord is a helpful expression of devotion and gratitude.

4. **Through spiritual gifts:** In hundreds of churches, drawn from a variety of different denominations, the use of spiritual gifts has acquired a new prominence. In such churches the regular use of the gift of tongues, with accompanying interpretation, as outlined in 1 Corinthians 14 by the apostle Paul, has become a significant means of stimulating communal worship of God. Other gifts such as prophecy, words of knowledge, and

encouragement have also taken their place in corporate worship. Healing services have also become a regular feature in the most unlikely church situations.

AVOIDING THE PITFALLS OF WORSHIP

As with every good thing, there are some pitfalls that we must be careful to avoid. The growth of free expression in worship can easily lead to dangers. If these are not avoided, Satan can succeed in directing large numbers of the people of God up a spiritual cul-de-sac from which they will not easily escape. These include:

Overenthusiasm. I once found myself sitting on the platform at a meeting while a woman danced up the aisle. A few moments later another followed suit. One woman appeared to allow her love for the Lord to be expressed naturally through her dance, but the other looked suspiciously as if she was trying to draw attention to herself. We need to watch our motives and remember Paul's gentle words of censure. "Everything must be done in a proper and orderly way" (1 Cor. 14:40, GNT).

Spiritual superiority. In certain circles, spiritual worth is measured by whether one speaks in tongues, raises hands, dances, or not! Such attitudes are dangerously immature.

Paul precedes his instructions to behave correctly with these words. "Desire earnestly to prophesy; and do not forbid to speak with tongues" (1 Cor. 14:39, NKJV). Yet nowhere in Scripture is there any teaching that those who do not speak in tongues are spiritually second-class citizens!

The purpose of this gift is to enable us to praise God when we become speechless with wonder in worshiping Him. Often as we share with the Lord all that we feel about Him, we discover that we run out of words, so He simply adds some to our praise.

Paul encourages the Corinthians to hold in balance their use of this gift of praying in the Spirit with praying in the mind. He insists that both are fruitful and that the former is not superior to the latter or vice versa.

Paul's deepest concern is expressed thus: "Since you are eager to have the gifts of the Spirit, you must try above everything else to make greater use of those which help to build up the church" (1 Cor. 14:12, GNT).

Self-centeredness. On the one hand we can become too immersed in fulfilling our own desires, and on the other we can be too concerned with what others are doing.

In the latter case we concentrate so much on the actions and attitudes of those around us that we can easily become guilty of neglecting the One who is the true focus of our worship. Things that are good in themselves can be carried to an unfortunate extreme. It is possible to overemphasize our freedom in worship to the detriment of other things.

This is especially true in the area of spiritual gifts. We must not seek to recover a necessary emphasis on the Spirit's present-day ministry among us at the expense of paying proper attention to His eternal character. If we concentrate too much on our own sense of spiritual excitement rather than what God wants to do through our lives, then the result can be that we can find ourselves emphasizing the gifts and neglecting the Giver!

It is never enough to sit on the fence enjoying our own worship. Nor is it right to spend our time passing judgment on the different styles of worship among us. Instead we must bring to the One who gave everything to us the offering of our lips and our lives. In other words, we worship God both in what we say and in how we live. Let us spend less of our time in examining the worship of others and more on asking whether our own is acceptable to God.

THOUGHT FOR THE DAY

So then, my brothers, because of God's great mercy to us I appeal to you: Offer yourselves as a living sacrifice to God, dedicated to his service and pleasing to him. This is the true worship that you should offer.

—ROMANS 12:1, GNT

WAIT A MINUTE

To worship God is not just to sing songs at a Sunday service. Jesus has created us to worship Him with our whole lives, in everything we do. If we are filled with the Spirit, then our worship should become a way of life. We then offer our bodies as living sacrifices to God, because this is a spiritual act of worship!

So we submit to His divine will to work through us by His Spirit, and our earthly bodies become vehicles for God's service. This then is worship—God is glorified through what we say and do, and the Holy Spirit helps us to live this way. He gives us a daily refreshing, enabling us to live to praise and worship God continuously.

Questions to Contemplate

1. In what further ways could you express your worship to God—meditating on Scripture, prayer, praise, spiritual gifts, dance, and so on?

2. Have you tried offering yourself to the Lord as a spiritual act of worship—a vessel for Him to use?

Space to Reflect

How might we better worship God with our whole life?

A Time to Pray

Father, please help me to understand true worship and all that it means for my life. Help me then to worship You in Spirit and truth, and on a daily basis. Amen.

THE MISSION:
CHURCH BEYOND BORDERS

*I*F IT WERE possible for any one of us to shrink the population of Planet Earth down to a small village that consisted of precisely one hundred people, then I sometimes wonder exactly what it would look like.

So often we imagine that it must parallel the society that we live in now. It proves to be very hard to think outside of the box.

Such an enormous group of people is going to be drawn together out of every "kindred, tribe, and nation" and into one great family. So we are called to a community, not just to a local fellowship, to be part of the global people of God. We are not only called, but we are also reborn into a family that extends worldwide and will never end.

The phrase "the church" used in Acts 8:1 provides us with just one example among many used to describe this body of believers. In this context, the only qualification for this principle was geographical, so it is the church at Colossae, Corinth, or Ephesus that is being referred to. No other distinction or division is made.

In this sense we can honestly conclude that together we join to form that many-member, corporate bride for which Jesus will return. Then we can begin to recognize what is involved in our desire to belong to each other and discover what it means to become a part of one another and to be the people of God. In those days our own petty nationalism will break down as we learn what it means to be one body in Christ Jesus.

WHERE THE SPIRIT MOVES

Some people might be offended if I were to suggest that conditions in Southern Sudan are reminiscent of a bygone era in the rest of the world, and yet that assessment would be true. A country that is approximately the size of Western Europe possesses only ten miles of paved roads.[1]

The first time I arrived at the remote village of Leithnomh I was greeted by one or two inquisitive onlookers as our little plane bounced along an apology for an airstrip. To call it a runway would involve stretching human credulity beyond acceptable limits.

Not only was the landing strip primitive, but also the village and its population were clearly suffering, and many exhibited a whole host of symptoms related to chronic malnutrition and serious deprivation. The first problem was that we were not expected. It was the middle of a period of such extreme famine that the vast majority of the people were simply concentrating on the need to survive.

Walking through the village, I noticed that about two hundred people had gathered together and were sitting on the ground underneath a spreading tree. Now anyone who knows Africa will appreciate that this usually indicates a religious meeting. Being inquisitive, I paused to ask the people what they were doing.

The reply was instantaneous.

"We are worshiping Jesus."

Then came their immediate question to me. "Have you ever heard of Him?"

No sooner had I replied than I had the next inquiry. "We've heard that there is a book about Him. Have you ever seen one?"

Before we were allowed to conduct a food assessment and begin to look together at ways in which we could begin to meet their physical needs, we first had to respond to their insistence that we provide them with Bibles.

It is no great surprise that a few months later more than one thousand people were baptized from that village and the surrounding area.

After the building of a school, the construction of a small hospital, the provision of initial veterinary services, and initial training of lay leaders for the emerging church, the air force of the Islamic fundamentalist Northern Sudanese government in Khartoum systematically and regularly bombed the village over a period of several weeks. The prime targets were the church and the World Relief compound.

In another part of Southern Sudan, the villages in the area of South Bor witnessed the sudden conversion of over 90 percent of the population in a period of just a few weeks. As in Leithnomh, it has proved difficult to discover any agent of direct human involvement in the process. There was no visiting evangelist involved, nor did those areas possess a single church or local pastor. The absence of a missionary or evangelistic initiative should not serve to make us skeptical as to the effectiveness of this work. The annals of church history are riddled with illustrations of times when the Holy Spirit has chosen to intervene suddenly, and sovereignly, in human affairs. What makes it even stranger is the way in which so often this direct intervention of the Holy Spirit comes on behalf of those who are among the poorest of the poor.

Many have commented that what is taking place today in Southern Sudan is reminiscent of the way in which the Spirit of God chose to take action at certain times of human desperation during the nineteenth and early twentieth centuries. These "baby" Christians may well be spiritually immature and largely ignorant of Scripture, but this is scarcely surprising in the light of the almost total absence of pastors or trained leaders. What is needed is food, medicine, Bibles, support, and encouragement to know that the rest of the family has not forgotten them!

CHANGE FROM ABOVE

Today we are all affected by global problems. Television and radio have removed our ignorance. Besieged by newsreel pictures of the poverty, starvation, and death of thousands each day, we can no longer claim that we are just not aware of what is going on. Gross economic inequality is coupled with political oppression as people are denied fundamental human rights by totalitarian regimes of left and right alike.

For far too long we have been prepared to give credence to the idea that the anointing that comes from the Holy Spirit is a matter of what we can receive for us—it is not. The Holy Spirit brings us power, not that we might vaunt ourselves, but in order that we might serve others with the love of Jesus.

The anointing that God provides for His servants is fundamentally about what the Holy Spirit is doing in our lives, not for ourselves, but in order that we might give of the very best for others.

We are not meant to tenaciously limp our way toward heaven; instead, the Holy Spirit is given to first empower us in order that we may play our part in seeing a little of this world changed for the Lord Jesus.

We need to ask ourselves whether our generosity stops at home or whether it extends overseas as well. Many agencies do provide the evangelical churches of the United States with a wonderful opportunity to demonstrate that we still believe that we are only a part of the church universal. Where our brothers and sisters in other parts of the world need our help, we should be happy to demonstrate what it means to belong to another kingdom.

THOUGHT FOR THE DAY

In the same way, faith by itself, if it is not accompanied by action, is dead.

—JAMES 2:17

WAIT A MINUTE

It may seem like an obvious statement, maybe even a frustrating one, but the fact is that we cannot just believe and not do anything about it! It is so easy for us to sit back accepting the gospel message and not looking beyond our own backyard.

We need to really ask ourselves what is our attitude toward our brothers and sisters around the world. Are they so far away that you find it difficult to see them as part of your family? It is definitely easier said than done.

QUESTIONS TO CONTEMPLATE

1. What does the concept of a global family really mean to you?

2. Do you need to look at your "good works" relating to them?

SPACE TO REFLECT

How might we combat the apathy in our Christian lives?

A TIME TO PRAY

Lord, help me not just to believe in You but to know what to do for You. Amen.

THE UNITY:
Working Together in God

*I*T HAS OFTEN been pointed out that although we can choose our friends, we are not at liberty to choose our relatives. Nowhere is this truer than in the church. We have no rights or privileges in the selection of our Christian brothers or sisters. It is a simple fact that from the moment we surrender the control of our lives to Jesus Christ, He not only comes to live within us by His indwelling Holy Spirit, but now He also incorporates us into His family, the church.

It is possible to be so captivated by the joy of personal conversion and the reality of God now living with us that we ignore, or choose to forget, the truth that we have suddenly acquired millions of brothers and sisters whom we have never met before. We will never escape from them, for we have been reborn into God's forever family.

As is the case in most (if not all) families, we will rarely agree on everything. This is especially true for relatively less important issues. It is possible to disagree over mutually exclusive styles of worship, forms of baptism, and methods of church government but still retain the vital acknowledgment of our sense of shared identity. These matters may be significant for us as individuals, but the Holy Spirit is always seeking to enable us as Christians to live alongside those who don't see these issues in quite the same way. That can prove to be a tough job!

Jesus did not want the church to be split by disagreements, gossip, or any other problems; His heart was that His followers would be "one." The Godhead is in complete unity and submission to one another, and Jesus wants the same for His church. In order for the Lord to display His nature and pure glory, and work powerfully and effectively through us, His body on earth must be in unity with one another, loving, supporting, and encouraging each other in everything.

The Puritan preacher Richard Baxter frequently quoted the following old saying, concerning the way in which we should respect one another's viewpoint, especially when it happens to differ from our own. This suggestion was that our attitude should be:

In matters non-essential, Liberty;
In matters essential, Unity;
But in all things, Charity.[1]

Put more simply, we might not have chosen each other or always approve of one another or always see things the same way, but we certainly are never allowed to reject others who are part of the same family.

ONE BODY IN CHRIST

In John 17, four times Jesus pleaded with His Father on behalf of His disciples and those who would follow that "they might be one."

The repetition only serves to reinforce how important this was to Jesus. He longed that we might know what it means to love and support each other. This was not just because He thought that it would be a good way to ensure the survival of the church, but also because it fell directly in line with the will of His Father.

Each individual will be different, but the Spirit will glory in uniting our variety. Jesus did not come to this planet to create a community of spiritual identical twins. He never intended to die in order to make us all the same as each other, but He did die to make us into a family, and that is what church is all about.

Time and again Jesus spoke and acted in order to gain a people for Himself who would one day be His love gift to His Father. Their unity together would then illustrate His own oneness with the other two members of the Trinity.

It is there that God will be the host while Jesus is the bridegroom and we as the church will be the bride of Jesus Christ. So heaven will be a corporate experience. We will not be alone but part of a vast company drawn from past, present, and future. We will come from every culture, race, and corner of the globe. For heaven will not be limited to those we like, those we would expect to be there, or those who are like us. It will be the entire company of the saints—all those who know and love Jesus.

Heaven will then itself be the location of the final wedding feast in human history.

THOUGHT FOR THE DAY

I will remain in the world no longer, but they are still in the world, and I am coming to you. Holy Father protect them by the power of your name—the name you gave me—so that they may be one as we are one.

—JOHN 17:11

WAIT A MINUTE

The enemy is constantly seeking to destroy relationships in the church. He often begins with our closest friends, sowing seeds of doubt in our minds. He plans to turn us against each other, spreading bitterness, envy, and hatred into our lives.

However, the Holy Spirit wants to work the opposite. He desires to encourage unity in the body of believers. He desires that we love one another as He seeks to spread truth among us. He knows that this will transform the ministry of the church, making ties so strong that others are drawn to it (Acts 3:42–47).

QUESTIONS TO CONTEMPLATE

1. Would you say that in your local congregation members tolerate problems between each other? If so, why? What can be done to restore relationships?

2. Do you allow others to negatively influence your opinion of people? How can you correct your thinking?

SPACE TO REFLECT

Consider James 3. Ask the Lord to show you the importance of unity in His church and how you can encourage it among your friends and acquaintances.

A TIME TO PRAY

Father, I pray that Your Spirit will help me to love my brothers and sisters no matter what they do to hurt me or my friends. Make me quick to forgive and strong to love. Amen.

THE ACTION:
WAITING FOR GOD

BUD HANCOCK, AN acquaintance of mine, sent me an account of an encounter that happened to his brother-in-law with the request that I might share it with others. Bud's brother-in-law had met two friends at a quaint restaurant. As he gazed out the window, he spotted what appeared to be a homeless man, carrying all of his worldly goods with a well-worn sign that read, "I will work for food."

Those who had taken notice of him shook their head in a mixture of sadness and disbelief. The men finished their meal and went their separate ways. As Bud's brother-in-law went about running errands, he felt the Spirit of God speaking to him, "Don't go back to the office until you've driven around town at least once more." With some hesitancy, he did and found the homeless man standing on the steps of a storefront church. The two began a dialogue, and he invited the stranger to lunch. It did not take long to discover that the stranger, whose name was Daniel, came from Florida and was on his way to St. Louis, Missouri. He had been traveling for the last fourteen years. Here begins Bud's brother-in-law's recounting of that divine appointment.

> I knew I had met someone unusual. We sat across from each other in the same restaurant I had left earlier. His face was weathered slightly beyond his thirty-eight years. His eyes were dark yet clear, and he spoke with an eloquence and articulation that was startling. He removed his jacket to reveal a bright red T-shirt that said, "Jesus is the Never Ending Story."
>
> Then Daniel's story began to unfold. He had seen rough times early in his life. He had made some wrong choices and reaped the consequences. Fourteen years earlier, while backpacking across the country, he had stopped on the beach in Daytona. He tried to get a job with some men who were putting up a large tent and some equipment, and concluded that they must be getting ready preparing for a concert. He was hired. But this was no concert; these men were preparing the venue for a series of revival meetings. During the services he began to see himself from a different

perspective, and he gave his life over to God.

"Nothing's been the same since," he said. "I felt the Lord telling me to keep walking and so I did. It's been some fourteen years now."

"Ever think of stopping?" I asked.

"Oh, once in a while, when it seems to get the best of me. But God has given me this calling. I give out Bibles. That's what is in my sack. I work to buy food and Bibles, and I give them out when His Spirit leads me to do so."

I sat there feeling totally amazed. My homeless friend was not homeless in the normal sense of the word; he was on a mission, and he lived this way by choice. One question burned inside me for a moment, and then I asked: "What's it like...to walk into a town carrying all your things on your back, and to show your sign?"

"Oh, it was humiliating at first. People would stare and make comments. Once someone tossed a piece of half-eaten bread and made a gesture that certainly didn't make me feel welcome. But then it became humbling to realize that God was using me to touch lives and change people's concepts of other folks like me."

My concept was changing, too. We finished our dessert and gathered his things. Just outside the door, he paused. He turned to me and said, "Come ye blessed of my Father and inherit the kingdom I've prepared for you. For when I was hungry you gave me food, when I was thirsty you gave me drink, a stranger and you took me in."

They parted, promising to pray for each other, but up until the time of this writing have never seen each other again. The plain and simple fact of the family is that one day there will be a reunion. For these two are heading for eternity together!

LOOKING FOR RENEWAL

The great thing is that when we least expect Him the Holy Spirit can turn up in such dramatic ways. Rarely does He do what we would have anticipated, but He does require that we are always alert and ready for Him to come in power.

Often we have come to describe the corporate activity of the Holy Spirit in the single word—*revival*. Some have even come to confidently announce that this will be taking place at their church on one particular evening in the immediate future. Unfortunately the Holy Spirit rarely proves to be so predictable!

We may well need to start to distinguish between three corporate activities of the Holy Spirit that are often confused with each other.

1. Renewal, or when the Holy Spirit comes to reenergize and revitalize the people of God

2. Revival, when God moves in power, bringing large numbers of unbelievers to Himself

3. Awakening, seen when not just the church is set on fire with spiritual power or when sinners are converted, but when society itself is transformed

All this God does through the Holy Spirit, and far more!

AMERICA TODAY

So just what is the spiritual condition of America in the early years of the twenty-first century?

I have heard many people tell me how desperately weak and spiritually poor they feel the United States is now, especially in comparison to the past.

Both America and Europe are rapidly becoming congested with four nations where the growth of pornography, unrestricted abortion, and occult practices has reached unprecedented peaks. Meanwhile, right now the rest of the world is experiencing the greatest move of God in the whole history of the church. One Korean congregation now tops 800,000 members and continues to grow. During the twentieth century alone Latin America witnessed a total of 50,000 believers in 1900 rise to estimated figures of around 100 million by the end of that century.[1] That kind of phenomenal growth was also paralleled in large parts of Africa. Still, Western Europe seems so strangely devoid of spiritual life.

Could it be that the living God is simply waiting for timid, frightened Christians hiding away in our cozy evangelical ghettoes, praying for survival, to begin to call on Him for the kind of blessing that is currently being witnessed in much of the third world?

This is one reason why I believe that the fantastic growth of prayer groups in the last decade is such a wonderful harbinger of all that God could still do among us, for more than three hundred years ago the great Puritan scholar Matthew Henry observed the fact that "when God intends great mercy for his people he gets them a-praying."

THOUGHT FOR THE DAY

Forget the former things; do not dwell on the past. See, I am doing a new thing! Now it springs up; do you not perceive it? I am making a way in the desert and streams in the wasteland...to give drink to my people.

—ISAIAH 43:18–20

WAIT A MINUTE

Have we lost our hunger for God to move in power? Are we so far removed from the Spirit of God that we struggle to hear His voice and direction? Isaiah tried to change the focus of his listeners; he wanted them to realize that God was trying to change their focus. He was attempting to make them see what the Lord was doing among them. He did not want them to dwell on other things past or present. He did not want them to carry on walking blindly. Instead his goal was to make people see that God was still at work.

Praise God that this is still a message for us today. His Holy Spirit is still at work among us. He is still crying out for us to perceive what He is doing and to actively respond.

QUESTIONS TO CONTEMPLATE

1. What is driving you?

2. Is it an inner longing to see and hear what the Lord is doing and to make a marked response, or do you lack that spiritual hunger?

SPACE TO REFLECT

Consider the real life encounter between Bud Hancock's brother-in-law and Daniel. Would you have had the same response to the Spirit of God and gone to look for him? Does anything need to change?

A TIME TO PRAY

Lord, I want to know the power of Your Spirit in a way that will prevent me from ever being a comfortable, oblivious Christian again. Amen.

DAY 42

THE POOR AND THE KINGDOM

*I*T WAS NO accident that the early church became strong among the poor and disenfranchised of society. The compassion revealed by His church was going to be the means of demonstrating the commitment of a Jesus who came to bring good news to the poor and the dispossessed (Luke 4:18–19). The Jerusalem church was rooted in the poorest parts of the city, and right from the start the lifestyle of the early Christians was intended to reveal the manner in which the Holy Spirit took hold of ordinary people and transformed their lives. Their witness would be the very means by which so many others would be brought to Jesus.

To most of them this would have been perfectly consistent with what they knew of the Lord. God had declared war on poverty. We might feel uncomfortable about that statement. We may feel that it is either too blunt or too political. But the Old Testament is unequivocal in announcing that the living God was against a society where poverty was tolerated. It was a command rather than a prophecy when He instructed Israel, "Not one of your people will be poor" (Deut. 15:4, GNT).

Jesus lived in a state of relative poverty, and He had some pretty tough things to say to the rich. It is always important to remember that it was when Zacchaeus offered generous compensation to those from whom he had embezzled and extorted money that Jesus could exclaim, "Salvation has come to this house today" (Luke 19:9, GNT).

Jesus also pointed out that the problems of wealth make it "much harder for a rich person to enter the Kingdom of God than for a camel to go through the eye of a needle" (Mark 10:25). No longer were social privilege and income a qualification for spiritual superiority. The fact that "good news is preached to the poor" (Matt. 11:5) was sent as a message by Jesus to John the Baptist to convince him, once and for all, that the Messiah had indeed arrived!

HOW THEN SHOULD THE CHURCH LIVE?

If this was the attitude of Jesus, then it is reasonable to ask the question as to how the Holy Spirit intends the church to be living and operating today.

It is important to note the way that Mary's song, the Magnificat, associates the spiritually poor and the spiritually hungry. The hungry and thirsty whom God satisfies are those who "hunger and thirst for righteousness." Such spiritual hunger and thirst is a characteristic of all God's people because our ultimate desires are spiritual and not material. While pagans are engrossed in the pursuit of possessions, Christians are truly to be different. Our quest is for God's kingdom and righteousness, which is what we are instructed to "seek first" (Matt. 6:33).

Are we more concerned about life at home? A culture that lives for designer labels can be very seductive. Do we flaunt our wealth with large houses, new cars, and the latest fashion trend? Are we guilty of judging people by external appearances? Do we enjoy controlling others and even seek power, or do we practice downward mobility and allow our lives to focus on love and concern for those who have fewer material possessions than ourselves?

The problem is that some of us will be tempted to tune out at this point. We feel tempted to react to the idea of being put on a guilt trip. Yet the real issue does not lie in condemning ourselves for the good things that God has provided for us. It is not a question of what we possess; that does not demonstrate what it means to be part of the family. But what we are prepared to give to others sends out a very different message from the Spirit to our world.

We may not feel comfortable in reading these words. Perhaps they spring from a political bias or envy of what God has given to others. We do need to face up to the reality that a society that equates a good standard of living with an individual's disposable income is sadly out of kilter with what Jesus had to say on the matter. He pointed out the inconsistency in the idea that Christianity and materialism can ever be comfortable bedfellows when He observed that, "No one can serve two masters.... You cannot serve both God and money" (Matt. 6:24).

So is it wrong for us to be relatively rich? Ultimately, for the Christian it is not a matter of what we have but how we put to good use what God has given us. For it is not really ours! If we have given our lives to Jesus, then that will include all our possessions, which we now hold in trust for Him. The Holy Spirit does not only want to direct our praise but also how we use the resources that God has entrusted to us.

If we only use them as He directs us, then there is actually no reason to feel guilty about what we have. It is only a gift from God and belongs to Him anyway. We should never be ashamed of what He has trusted us to steward for Him, nor should we despise it. But we should hold lightly to what we have, recognizing that He can lay claim to whatever part He wants at any moment that He chooses.

Never feel guilty over what we have, only about our reluctance to give it away!

What will always be far more important than any feelings of guilt or remorse will be our attitude toward our possessions and the generosity of spirit with which we are prepared to dispose of them when we receive divine instructions through the prompting of the Holy Spirit.

THOUGHT FOR THE DAY

The King will reply, "...whatever you did for one of the least of these brothers of mine, you did for me."

—MATTHEW 25:40

WAIT A MINUTE

We are called to recognize the poor and to respond. The anointing of the Holy Spirit is given to us so that we can take good news to the poor. The Holy Spirit calls us to give, love, and pray for those who are worse off than ourselves in this country and across the world. Jesus' life clearly demonstrated the importance of giving and loving the poor of the world. He desires that we take up His mantle, not only to verbally share the good news of Christ, but also to let our actions demonstrate the knowledge we have of His love.

QUESTIONS TO CONTEMPLATE

1. Where do your priorities lie?

2. Are there any groups of people in your neighborhood who need you to serve them, and how can you start?

SPACE TO REFLECT

Is your heart on fire with love for the needy of the world? The Lord gave Himself for others; let Him remind us of His heart for the poor and needy (1 John 3:17) and break ours with the same compassion.

A TIME TO PRAY

Lord, please forgive us as Your church for sometimes preferring the rich to the poor. Help us to live as a serving church, devoting our lives to the ministry of Your love to those who have less than ourselves. And individually, I ask that Your Spirit will always give me the desire to love, give, and pray for others, and not just to concentrate on myself. Amen.

WEEK SEVEN

LIVING BY THE SPIRIT

An enemy has done this…Satan has opposed the doctrine of the Spirit-filled life about as bitterly as any other doctrine there is. He has confused it, opposed it, and surrounded it with false notions and fears. He has blocked every effort of the church of Christ to receive from the Father her divine and blood-bought patrimony. The church has tragically neglected this great liberating truth—that there is now for the child of God a full and wonderful and completely satisfying anointing with the Holy Ghost.

—A. W. TOZER

THE ANOINTING:
BUT FOR WHAT?

EVERY DAY WE witness the saving love of Jesus and the transforming power of His Spirit in our lives. We can only live and speak as the Spirit enables us. But God also intends His people to demonstrate His power in the world. He calls us to specific acts of ministry and service, which demand a special empowering from the Holy Spirit.

Throughout the Old Testament we read about the Holy Spirit "coming upon" people to prepare them for service. But in the New Testament, the Holy Spirit comes to live "within" the lives of God's people.

As D. L. Moody observed, "When the Spirit came to Moses, the plagues came upon Egypt, and he had power to destroy men's lives. When the Spirit came upon Elijah, fire came down from heaven. When the Spirit came upon Joshua, he moved around the city of Jericho, and the whole city fell into his hands. But when the Spirit came upon the Son of Man, He gave His life, He healed the broken-hearted."

The Holy Spirit may well live "within" us, but He still comes "upon" us to anoint our lives for particular acts of service. Without that anointing, our labors for God can never attain their full potential. Day by day we need to know the Holy Spirit's filling and anointing on our lives. Then, and only then, can we join Jesus in saying:

> The Spirit of the Lord is upon me, because he has chosen me to bring good news to the poor. He has sent me to proclaim liberty to the captives and recovery of sight to the blind; to set free the oppressed and announce that the time has come when the Lord will save his people.
>
> —LUKE 4:18–19

We are anointed:

- To live a new life
- For suffering
- For blessing
- To heal

 To deliver

 To bring good news to the poor

Anointed to live a new life

At this point many new believers encounter incredible difficulties. It is great to receive divine salvation, but what are we really supposed to be saved from? What is this new life into which the Holy Spirit is supposed to be leading us?

The easiest response is to suggest that, in effect, we have been delivered from lifestyle and a particular culture in order to be transposed into another. Now that may seem easy and straightforward, but it is a very difficult position to justify from Scripture. The Bible would seem to adopt the understanding that we are forgiven sinners called to continue living within the world, not attempting to escape from it. The reason is that we would be in the right place to encourage others to respond to the calling of divine love.

In other words, the blessings we have received are not only given to us for the purpose of our own comfort and enjoyment. They are given in order that we might share them with others. For our faith was always given to us in the anticipation that the Holy Spirit would then enable us to give it away to others.

Anointed for suffering

We are not promised an easy life. The Holy Spirit has come to make us into the hands and feet of Jesus, the One who won us with His "suffering love." He suffered and died to bring us to Himself, and He requires our own self-giving love in return (1 Cor. 13:4). God matures us and teaches us to share in the suffering of others, not by providing us with an easy life, but by exposing us to the sorrows and pressures of life. When we discover our own Spirit-given capacity to endure tribulation, we learn what it means to be worthy of God's calling on our lives (Heb. 12:5–11).

Anointed for blessing

While we must remember that we are not immune from the challenges in this life, which the Holy Spirit helps us to overcome, we must not go to the other extreme—that we cannot be blessed in the here and now. We must maintain a balance, knowing that we will suffer in this world, but that the Holy Spirit also brings an anointing to bless.

When God wants to bless His people, He follows no man-made prescription, and we should be ready to receive absolutely any blessing that He wants to shower upon us. What often proves to be more difficult is to rejoice with others when the Lord chooses to bless them but denies the blessing to us.

Anointed to heal

Although healing should remain our expectation and hope, we must be careful to encourage faith, not foolishness. We must first seek to find God's will and then act in obedience to that will rather than our own desires, however good they may be!

We operate in Jesus' name, in the Holy Spirit's anointing, and only under His authority. God tells us what to do, not vice versa. Healing can be progressive or instantaneous. The Lord responds to faith, not familiarity.

Anointed to deliver

The authority of His Holy Spirit is for Jesus alone to give:

> I have given you authority to trample on snakes and scorpions and to overcome all the power of the enemy; nothing will harm you.
> —LUKE 10:19

We will cover deliverance in depth in tomorrow's entry. But for now, you need to know that you have been anointed and appointed with divine authority to defeat your enemy.

Anointed to bring good news to the poor

The biblical phrase "Come out from among them, and be ye separate, saith the Lord" (2 Cor. 6:17, KJV) has too often become a "catch-all" license excusing evangelical Christians from having to maintain any contact with the rest of humankind.

Contrary to the opinions of many, Christianity is an inclusive religion, not an exclusive one. Jesus came to the world to share His message of hope with ordinary people. His Holy Spirit has anointed us in order that we might be equipped to live in our world, and not seek to avoid it. We are anointed to represent the cause of Christ to our world and not merely attempt to preserve our own sense of personal purity.

THOUGHT FOR THE DAY

The Spirit of the Lord came upon him in power so that he tore the lion apart with his bare hands as he might have torn a young goat.
—JUDGES 14:6

WAIT A MINUTE

Sometimes we can get easily confused with the role of the Holy Spirit in our lives. We don't always understand why He "dwells in" our lives and still "comes upon" us at various times. The distinction between the Holy Spirit coming "in" or "on" a person is not a rigid one that we should have solved!

In the Old Testament the Spirit came "upon" people. In the New Testament the Spirit comes to live "in" all God's people. However, in the New Testament the Spirit still comes "on" the believers at Pentecost to anoint them to share the good news and ultimately turn the world upside down. The difference is that while His presence within us is permanent, His anointing that comes upon us is not. Without the anointing our labors will never attain their greatest potential. We will need His filling and anointing at all times.

QUESTIONS TO CONTEMPLATE

1. Have you struggled to grasp the distinction between the Spirit coming "into" your life and coming "upon" you?

2. Can you then be aware of the Spirit's anointing for specific tasks?

SPACE TO REFLECT

Reflect on Samson in Judges (13:25; 14:6; 19; 15:14; 16:20) and David (Ps. 51:11). Compare with the early chapters in Acts to create a deeper understanding of the Spirit's role in our lives.

A TIME TO PRAY

Father, thank You that Your Spirit lives in me. I pray that I will know Your anointing more and more, so that I will always achieve my potential in serving You most effectively. Amen.

DAY 44

THE DELIVERANCE:
WHERE DEMONS MUST FLEE!

THOSE WHO ENJOYED the fictional cinematic trilogy of *The Lord of the Rings* will appreciate the sense of visual horror that we would have if we could see the ghastly forces that form the nucleus of Satan's demon forces (Matt. 12:22–29; Luke 8:30–38; Rev. 16:13–14). Mercifully they remain invisible, so we are spared the sight of them, but this does not make them to be any less real.

Having unequivocally conquered Satan through His death on the cross, Jesus now equips His people, by His Spirit, to live in triumph over their vanquished enemy and his defeated minions.

We could spend many pages just looking at this subject, but here are some brief guidelines as to how we can confront any direct assault against us or see deliverance come to anyone who truly seeks freedom in Jesus.

1. Never go looking for demons. Don't imagine the demonic where it doesn't exist; don't let your mind and imagination dictate. Listen to the voice of your spirit—and the witness of others.

2. Distinguish carefully between levels of demonic activity: demonized, oppressed, or in the rare situation, possessed.

3. Be careful to distinguish between psychiatric or psychological disorder, which can be fostered by Satan and demonic activity.

4. Don't act alone; beware of being impetuous.

5. Don't lay hands on the demonized. Rebuke in Jesus' name and realize that the void must be filled and damage healed by the Holy Spirit (Luke 11:25).

6. Warn fellow Christians to avoid any association at all with areas of occultism: for example, horoscopes, psychic arts, séance, astral projection, and so on.

7. Be careful not to give credit to Satan; don't get wrongly fascinated or interested, even under the guise of spiritual care. Exalt Jesus, and dismiss the devil!

It is important to avoid wasting time on those who have dabbled in the occult but have no desire to be freed from the results. There are six conditions for people to normally find true freedom:

1. Humility
2. Honesty
3. Confession of sin
4. Repentance
5. Forgiveness of all others
6. Calling on the name of the Lord

I hesitate even to mention this aspect of the Spirit's activity. We run grave risks of demanding knowledge that is generally frankly unhelpful. Too often people become excited about the idea of exploring this issue in depth. The great number of books on Satan and all his works speaks volumes of the fascination that the subject can hold, by Satan, for the people of God. I far prefer the attitude expressed in that phrase from Canon Michael Green, *I believe in Satan's downfall.* And that, one might say, is the end of that!

THOUGHT FOR THE DAY

Submit yourselves, then, to God. Resist the devil, and he will flee from you.

—JAMES 4:7

WAIT A MINUTE

We need to daily submit ourselves to God, taking up His armor for protection. We are called to oppose the devil, to refuse to go along with any of his plans or give in. We need to withstand the devil's schemes and learn to defend ourselves.

One of the key strategies the enemy likes to use is to get us to believe his lies that say we are not capable of serving our Lord or that sow seeds of doubt in us. With every lie from the devil there is a piece of truth that comes from our heavenly Father. Because He has the victory and we are His children, we can claim His truths for our lives. We can take a stand by refusing to believe anything the evil one tries to tell us and standing on the truth of what Jesus Himself tells us.

QUESTIONS TO CONTEMPLATE

1. Are there any obvious lies you are aware of in your life?

2. Have you accepted the truth that God is for you, not against you, and His words are the truth?

SPACE TO REFLECT

Refuse to let the devil hold you captive in your mind. You belong to the Lord Jesus, and therefore you have power, by His Spirit, to take a stand.

A TIME TO PRAY

Lord, help me to recognize the devil's schemes but not to be overly fascinated by them. Teach me to know when and where the enemy is at work in my life and in the lives of others, so that I can deal with it wisely and in Your strength. Amen.

THE PROCLAMATION:
ANOINTED TO WITNESS

THE EARLY CHURCH experienced incredible initial growth because ordinary people like you and me were empowered by the Holy Spirit to share the good news. These men and women did not use their own strength and resources in seeking to bring people to saving faith in Jesus Christ, nor was this just a message from the past for us to bless us. After Jesus' ascension into heaven, He left the power and presence of His Holy Spirit to fill the lives of His disciples who would have to remain on the earth.

So in the same way, when God attempts a mighty move upon a nation today, He does not reserve His resources and only make them available to some kind of spiritual elite. The Lord longs to take hold of each one of us in order that He might make us to be His messengers to our dying land. "Yes, even on my servants, both men and women, I will pour out my Spirit in those days, *and they will proclaim my message*" (Acts 2:18, GNT, emphasis added).

It is not for us to seize the rope and rescue ourselves. The Holy Spirit provides the rope, and our task is always to hand the rope to those suffering around us. He gives us the words to say and the authority with which to deliver them. He takes hold of insignificant, ordinary people to transform them into powerful witnesses for Jesus Christ with lives as well as words that speak the truth. It is our job to do the task that we have been given.

GOD'S GREAT EVANGELIST

It is a simple fact that the Holy Spirit is the supreme evangelist. He has been given to guide people toward the truth, because He is the Spirit of truth (John 14:17, 16:3; 1 John 4:6).

By this Spirit, people are convicted of sin. He is the author of new life and the One who brings us into the reality of being born into a new life in Jesus (John 16:7–8, 6:63, 3:6–8; 2 Cor. 3:6; 1 Pet. 3:18). He gives us the assurance of knowing that our salvation has been accomplished through crucified love and that it is secure (Rom. 8:16; Gal. 4:6; 1 John 3:2, 4:13, 5:6).

This same authority can, and will, apply to us when we are prepared to come to Jesus confessing our inability to serve effectively apart from the strength that His Spirit provides. The problems and blockages that get in the way and impede this flow of God's Spirit are all ours. They include:

☞ Our reluctance to share our faith

☞ Our failure to pray

☞ Our lack of love and compassion for those around us

☞ Our isolation from our community

☞ Our cowardice when we could have spoken

And, yet, into all of our failings, God can insert His Spirit, and when He does, nothing can ever be the same again. When we confess our inadequacy, when we stop trying to serve God with our human abilities, then we can plug into divine resources. Our words can be replaced by His, our life by His, our compassion by His, and our prayer life by His, and all this through the intervention of the Spirit of God Himself within our lives.

This was to be so vividly demonstrated on the Day of Pentecost. The new believers received the Holy Spirit at the moment of their conversion. Immediately they were added by the Holy Spirit to the infant church, began to share in its life and practices, and gave testimony to their newfound faith. The process then continued with the next batch of new believers, and so the church grew.

We might possess few resources within ourselves, but it is as we allow the Holy Spirit to control our lives that He reminds us of the message and provides the resources and encouragement for its delivery. No one would pretend that such lives are easy, but they are fruitful.

How to Make a Difference

One story from the nineteenth century will serve to illustrate the point. The great American evangelist D. L. Moody made a promise to God shortly after his conversion. He promised God that he would not allow twenty-four hours to pass without sharing Jesus. One night he realized that he had not kept his word. Hurrying out of bed, he feared that he would not meet anybody, but there, under a lamppost, stood a man.

He asked this perfect stranger, "Are you a Christian?"

The man, both embarrassed and antagonistic, answered with violent rejection and was also extremely offended—furthermore he said so! Finding out who Moody was, this man told others in no uncertain terms the damage that Moody had done.

Moody was crestfallen; what a mistake. Maybe he should be less blindly enthusiastic?

Now many of us could never take this course of action. But God honors the efforts of those who can, those to whom He has given that kind of opportunity, and who have been created by the Holy Spirit with the kind of character to take advantage of it.

> Weeks passed by. One night Mr. Moody was in bed when he heard a tremendous pounding at his front door. He jumped out of bed and rushed to the door. He thought the house was on fire. He thought the man would break down the door. He opened the door and there stood this man. He said, "Mr. Moody, I have not had a good night's sleep since that night you spoke to me under the lamppost, and I have come around at this unearthly hour of the night for you to tell me what I have to do to be saved." Moody was able to lead the man to Jesus. Soon afterwards the man died and, because of Moody's spiritual aggression, will spend eternity with Jesus Christ![1]

Such witness is not born in human enthusiasm; it comes directly from the Spirit of God.

THOUGHT FOR THE DAY

Even on my servants, both men and women, I will pour out my Spirit in those days, and they will prophesy.

—ACTS 2:18

WAIT A MINUTE

We do not minister to a dying world in our human strength.

The Holy Spirit is poured out on each one of us to equip us. That is why Jesus did not allow His disciples to step foot outside Jerusalem until they had received His Spirit.

Likewise we *must not* attempt to do the work of God out of our own resources because we will never see dramatic results, and our morale will drop very quickly. Without the Spirit coming upon the early believers, the church would be nowhere today. They may have convinced and argued people into the kingdom, but without the impartation of supernatural strength the gospel would not, and does not, spread at half the speed. The truth needs to be revealed by the Holy Spirit working throughout the world, or the truth can never be found. He provides the rope to help us to minister, and we, in turn, must pass it on to others.

QUESTIONS TO CONTEMPLATE

1. How can you take hold of the Spirit's rope of empower-
    ment to help in your witness?

2. Can you name three friends whom you would love to
    see come to Jesus?

SPACE TO REFLECT

Consider the early chapters in Acts. Ask God to pour out His Spirit
afresh on His church to make our witness as powerful as that of the early
believers.

A TIME TO PRAY

*Lord, please equip me with Your Spirit's strength every morn-
ing to make my witness powerful and uncompromising. Please
convict me when I try to share Your truth in my own strength,
and come to speak through me at all times. Amen.*

DAY 46

THE PAIN THAT PREPARES
FOR THE GLORY

*I*RMA IS ONE of those ladies who make it difficult to guess either her age or background. I do not even know the story of how she came to Jesus. I only know that she belongs to Him because of her response to the tragic events of January 13, 2001. None of Irma's neighbors could doubt her faith either in the face of such intense suffering.

It was around ten thirty in the morning when the earthquake struck. Irma was in her house with two others from the local church. Panic stricken at the severity of the quake, they stood and held hands together believing in that instant that the end of the world had come. Then they heard the noise like nothing that they had ever heard before. When the tremor stopped and the three of them left Irma's house, they gazed around at what remained of their middle-class neighborhood in San Salvador.

Looking up at the thickly wooded hillside that once overshadowed the dwellings, they realized with horror that about one-third of it was missing! The earthquake had dislodged the hillside, and the trees had come crashing down on this peaceful and unsuspecting San Salvadorian suburb. Some traveled almost a mile before landing in a kitchen or a bedroom. The rest of the hillside immediately became a landslide, as the dirt and rocks hurtled down to cover what remained of the houses. When the rescuers arrived, the area had become a vast communal graveyard with survivors milling around in a state of total bewilderment. Then there were those like Irma, whose houses stood on either side of the devastation, surveying the ravaged area in horror.

For the survivors and their friends and neighbors, it was a moment of total confusion. For Irma it was an opportunity, a chance to pray with those who stood there bewildered at all that had happened and to offer what help and support she could. Many Christians had died, including at least one pastor. Two church buildings were condemned to be demolished. But God's people were thinking of the sufferings of others, not of themselves. The distribution of food and clothing was swiftly arranged, and Irma moved in, under an anointing from her Lord, to minister to the needs of those who had lost everything they possessed. The end results of what was achieved in that and subsequent days will only be revealed in eternity.

CALLED TO ENDURE

My oldest daughter has a trademark way of closing any letter with the words, "Keep going." While it is certainly right to observe that while this is always tough when operating in our own strength, it is a clear function of the Holy Spirit to enable us to persevere and to "keep going." Naturally we prefer the good times to the tougher ones. Yet the reality of who we are is often revealed most clearly when we are under pressure.

As God's people we have been promised two things—success and suffering. At first glance, these may seem to be contradictory. Yet this success relates more to the future than to the present. This idea is often less than enthusiastically received in a modern world dependent on notions of "instant success." So the emerging popular belief among many evangelical Christians is that the physical and material blessings we have received indicate the degree to which we are actively walking with God and serving Him. Put in its crudest form, the idea is that our openness to the Holy Spirit can be measured in terms of the condition of our physical health and financial prosperity.

In light of Jesus' example it is exceptionally difficult to grasp one who denied Himself the comforts of a home and even took advantage of a (conveniently) floating fish in order to pay the tax bill (Matt. 8:20; 17:27). He continually emphasized the demands of sacrificial discipleship and promised His disciples that they must always expect to suffer in His cause, so we surely can have no reason to anticipate an easier ride today.

THOUGHT FOR THE DAY

I consider that our present sufferings are not worth comparing with the glory that will be revealed in us.

—ROMANS 8:18

WAIT A MINUTE

It is a scary thought to think that we have actually been promised suffering here on earth. For many of us living in the West, suffering is such a foreign concept for us because, in comparison to many parts of our world, we live with such minimal amounts of it. But suffering should not always be seen as purely negative; it can cause us to have greater dependence and trust in Christ (2 Cor. 1:8–12), and it strengthens and changes us for the better (Rom. 5:3–5). Paul also believed that our suffering was one strategy that the Holy Spirit used to prepare us for the glory ahead (Rom. 8:18; 2 Cor. 4:17–18). For one day we will reign with Christ.

QUESTIONS TO CONTEMPLATE

1. In the light of eternity, is suffering worthwhile when God walks there with you?

2. How do you view suffering?

SPACE TO REFLECT

How much do you think you are worth, and how is that value measured by the Lord?

A TIME TO PRAY

Lord, help me to be prepared to suffer as well as to enjoy myself. Teach me to live a lifestyle where I am willing to "lay down my life for my friends," as John 15:13 says. Amen.

THE HEALER:
Jesus Himself

Many years ago I was conducting a coffee bar mission in a London suburb. While praying with a group of local Christians on the morning before the mission was due to begin, there was a sudden interruption. A young nurse entered the room in tears. She had been longing to be involved in the mission. That morning her doctor had confirmed that she had perforated her eardrum. She would be unable to hear well enough in a coffee bar atmosphere to share her faith.

I can't explain why I reacted the way I did, except that I knew that this was not what God wanted. I urged the youth leader from a local Brethren assembly to stand with me and pray for the girl. Never before had I specifically prayed for healing for anyone. But she was healed! The youth leader was as surprised as I was, but he took things one step further—he married her!

I am myself married to a lady who has three times avoided imminent admission to hospital or actual surgery because she has been prayed for. Now Ruth just rejoices, while those of us doing the praying have sometimes had to review our theology in the light of what God has done.

HEALING WAS IMPORTANT TO JESUS

Healing was so prominent in the ministry of Jesus that many of us today might wonder at why Jesus spent so much valuable preaching time in this way. What made the practice of healing so very important in the ministry of Jesus?

1. Healing was an expression of the mind and will of God for humankind. Mark records the moment when "a man suffering from a dreaded skin disease came to Jesus, knelt down, and begged him for help. 'If you want to,' he said, 'you can make me clean.' Jesus was filled with pity, and reached out and touched him. 'I want to,' he answered. "Be clean!'" (Mark 1:40–41, GNT).

2. Healing was a sign of the compassion of Jesus. This is evidenced by the word that Mark employs for "pity." This word that is often used of the compassion of Jesus means a love that flows from the human intestines. It comes from the very depths of a man or woman. This is no surface reaction or response; it is a heartfelt compassion, what could genuinely be called a "gut-level love."

3. Healing was a fulfillment of prophecy: "He did this to make come true what the prophet Isaiah had said, 'He himself took our sickness and carried away our diseases'" (Matt. 8:17, GNT).

4. Healing brings glory to God: "He is blind so that God's power might be seen at work in him" (John 9:3, GNT).

5. Healing stimulates faith: "Believe me when I say that I am in the Father and the Father is in me. If not, believe because of the things I do" (John 14:11, GNT).

The actions that Jesus did and miracles performed in the power of the Spirit were way beyond the human imagination. Furthermore, the Lord Jesus promised that we could expect to see even greater works happen in the future (John 14:12). Rather than just look back, He encouraged us to look forward as well, with both faith and anticipation that He will fulfill His promise through His Spirit.

POWER FOR TODAY

Power for Jesus, the early church, and indeed for Christians today is no wild, irrational thing. Obviously we cannot control God, but to some extent we do have a certain control over whether or not God's power may work through us. There are conditions that need to be fulfilled in us if the Holy Spirit is to move freely through our lives.

1. Motives are important. As Simon the sorcerer discovered, money could not purchase God's power. It is not just available for anyone. (See Acts 8:18–24.)

2. Prayer and fasting are sometimes the necessary preparation for God to empower His people. (See Mark 9:29.)

3. God's power is only available to His people and at His own initiative and intention. (See Luke 10:9, 21; Acts 5:12.)

4. The glory and honor must go to God, not to those He has used as His servants. (See Acts 3:9.)

5. It is important to be grounded in the body of Christ, to one another, to our role and function within the body, and to be rightly related to Jesus.

I have discovered over the years that God's actions are spontaneous. He rarely chooses to fit into the well-worn pathways that I have devised for Him. We operate in Jesus' name and only under His authority. Therefore we need to recognize that God does not respond to our own pet formulas. He tells us what to do, not vice versa.

There is real variety in what God does. God can call His people to endure suffering in order that He might fulfill His purposes. When the disciples tried to claim a monopoly on God's dealings, Jesus rebuked them. "John spoke up, 'Master, we saw a man driving out demons in your name, and we told him to stop, because he doesn't belong to our group.' 'Do not try to stop him,' Jesus said to him and to the other disciples, 'because whoever is not against you is for you'" (Luke 9:49–50, GNT).

THOUGHT FOR THE DAY

I tell you the truth, anyone who has faith in me will do what I have been doing. He will do even greater things than these, because I am going to the Father.

—JOHN 14:12

WAIT A MINUTE

The fact is that we struggle to really believe that these words are true for us today. Because we lack faith in ourselves and belief in the power of God, we find it almost impossible to grasp that we can do even greater things than Jesus Himself! This has been a problem throughout the centuries—so much so that we tend to ignore passages like these because we find them so hard to relate to. Yet the truth still stands; Jesus said that His followers would perform great miracles and have power to heal.

Jesus does the work through us by His Spirit. We do not have to strive to make someone well—it is up to God!

QUESTIONS TO CONTEMPLATE

1. Do you lack confidence to believe that God would use you to heal someone?

2. Do you believe Jesus when He says that you will do greater things than Him?

SPACE TO REFLECT

Allow Jesus to confirm in your heart today that He does want to use you for His glory and in powerful ways.

A TIME TO PRAY

Lord Jesus, help me to know when Your Spirit is directing me to pray for someone and to believe that You can move in power through me. Lord, help me not to be so far removed from the concepts of healings and miracles that I miss what You are trying to do. Amen.

THE FILLING:
ANOINTED FOR RENEWAL

*I*T SEEMS THAT contrasting beliefs about the role of the Holy Spirit in the lives of individual Christians have been the biggest single cause of internal division over the past thirty years.

At the epicenter of this controversy is the term "baptism with the Holy Spirit." The question relates to whether or not this can refer to a one-time instantaneous experience at some time after an individual has repented and been united with God through the Holy Spirit. If this is possible, then the second question emerges as to whether this is an essential spiritual experience for all believers. If it is, we need to ask if some are right in their insistence that the necessary evidence for this "baptism" is that one immediately speaks in other tongues.

We always need to be very careful to avoid insisting that everyone else needs to follow the same spiritual path by which God has led us as individuals. It is always vital to remember that to demand that all others should be like us is probably an indication of our personal insecurity rather than the divine intention. For the living God is perfectly able to lead His people by different routes to the same destination. The same caution should also apply to our use of words. In the New Testament, the phrase "baptism in the Holy Spirit" is often associated with repentance and faith as part of the conversion experience. Since then, those Christians who have come to a deeper experience of the Spirit after their conversion refer to this as a "baptism in the Holy Spirit." Because we use words in different ways, the danger is that we fail to understand each other.

We tend too easily to interpret Scripture in the light of our own personal experience. This leads to false feelings of spiritual superiority, as we then assume that we must be right and therefore everyone else is simply wrong. This is a very dangerous practice because it means that we place the power and intentions of God within the very narrow box of our own understanding. Often, instead of allowing others the liberty to search for that biblical experience of the Spirit that God has made available for them, we try to lead them into an experience that mimics our own.

MOVING FORWARD TOGETHER

Charismatic evangelicals and non-Charismatic evangelicals have this in common: they share an evangelical heritage that unites them in faith and experience in all areas other than an understanding of the Person and work of the Holy Spirit. But having seen where we can differ, let us now examine where, even on this issue, we have areas of surprisingly broad agreement.

1. We all agree that each one of us needs power from God with which to live the Christian life.

2. We all agree that this power is available to all of God's people, because each of us receives the Holy Spirit at conversion as the promise of all that He longs to achieve in each one of us.

3. We all agree that the Holy Spirit wants to achieve more in our lives than a mere unique experience. Paul's words to the Ephesian church, "be filled," were both a command and an instruction. More literally translated they read, "Continue to be being filled." In other words, they speak of a daily, ongoing release.

4. The Holy Spirit brings more than gifts to the people of God; He produces fruit in our lives.

The famed American evangelist Dwight L. Moody was once speaking to a nineteenth-century British congregation on this theme, and some, particularly among leaders and clergy, were offended by his words. Moody was taken to one side after the meeting and interrogated. "Why do you say that we need to go on being filled with the Holy Spirit? We've been filled twenty or thirty years ago. Why do we need to be filled again?"

Moody's reply was a classic of spiritual commonsense. "I need to be filled with the Spirit every moment of each day because I leak."[1]

We remain a very "leaky" people who desperately need to know God's reality in our experience today—not just in our memories!

A sense of holy dissatisfaction with the poverty of our knowledge of God and our love for Him would quickly transform the situation. No longer would we be content with merely knowing about God; we would hunger to know God, and not just by hearsay! In other words, we would demand a deep, intimate relationship. The Holy Spirit prompts that very desire in our hearts.

Argument and debate have proved inconclusive, but one thing is certain. Our spiritual hunger does not disappear, and God still does want to bless His people and provide for us all that we need.

Thought for the Day

Again Jesus said, "Peace be with you! As the Father has sent me, I am sending you." And with that He breathed on them and said, "Receive the Holy Spirit."

—John 20:21–22

Wait a Minute

Whatever happens for each one of us, we can be assured that the Lord will lead us down many different routes to the same destination. He may have given you a mighty encounter with, or baptism from, the Holy Spirit, or He may work in a much quieter fashion. You may speak in tongues, but you may not. Do not worry about what you personally experience of the Holy Spirit. As long as you ask Him, the Lord will fill you and anoint you with His Spirit to do His work.

Questions to Contemplate

1. Have you found yourself comparing your spiritual experiences with other people? Remember, your experience is valuable.

2. Whatever you call it, are you ready for whatever God wants to do in your life?

Space to Reflect

Allow God to reassure you that whatever His plan for your life, it does involve His Spirit, and He may not do what you expect!

A Time to Pray

Lord, thank You that You never work to a standard blueprint for everyone. I want Your Spirit to fill me and anoint me to do Your work. Help me not to limit the work of the Holy Spirit, but to be open to all that You want to do in my life. Amen.

DAY 49

THE COMPULSION TO
DO HIS WILL

ONE MINOR LEAGUE soccer club in England had become a bit of a joke. At one stage in a particularly disastrous season, they had half a dozen fixtures left and still hadn't won a game! The problem was that losing had grown to be so familiar and they had become so accustomed to failure that winning might have constituted a problem.

That same sense of failure can often result in our crashing down in our Christian lives. Time and again we act in good faith, responding to calls for a deeper commitment, only to fail and fail again. Promises, resolutions, and good intentions all to seem to be to no avail.

Jesus was completely different. He faced all the trials and temptations of life and yet remained totally consistent in following His Father's will. Throughout His time on earth, Jesus lived in complete obedience to the will of His Father. By so doing, He initiated a totally new era on earth.

Tragically, too many of us as Christians are content with what we are. For many, to be respected by their near neighbors and to live upright, kind, compassionate, and orthodox Christian lives appears to them to be more than sufficient. Too often they are simply trying to find God through their own intellects, to respond to Him with their own emotions, and to serve Him as an act of their own wills. The truth is that before we can know God, respond to Him, or serve Him, we need first to allow His Spirit to breathe new life into our spirits. Then our minds, our emotions, and our wills are driven by, motivated by, and submitted to the life of the Spirit of God.

We all need to be controlled not by our own selfish desires but by the Spirit. It is not enough to determine within our souls—mind, will, and emotions—that we will follow Christ. We must allow the whole of our lives to be determined by our spirit—our capacity to receive the Holy Spirit, to love God, and to live in His strength, not our own. Many preachers have affirmed that if they had not known about the dividing of spirit and soul, then it would be hard to imagine what the condition of their spiritual life would have been.

A Personal Discovery

Without doubt, one of the most crushing and humiliating experiences in our Christian lives is that awful moment when we realize that we have performed actions that, judged by our standards, were good but were not in the purpose and intention of God.

Even after overcoming basic sin, our spiritual battle has only just begun. Early victories come only with the Holy Spirit's help. Our ongoing struggle cannot be carried on in our own strength. "How can you be so foolish! You began by God's Spirit; do you now want to finish by your own power?" (Gal. 3:3, GNT).

The Spirit of God will never adapt Himself to our formula and reduce Himself to any process that we might feel would be appropriate for Him, however well motivated we might have been. He is God, and we are mere created beings. So He will not agree to fit into our well-worn pathways that we have carefully carved out for Him, even though we have spent so long planning every footprint.

Therefore, we must not presume that God will heal someone at the same time and place that we have decided He will. It may not happen then. It may not happen instantaneously. It may happen over time or even not at all. We need to entrust everything to God. Only He knows why, and it is only by the Spirit's grace that we see some of the picture.

We are called to seek God for His timing and His will so that we are not frequently disappointed. The danger is that we begin to plan something or establish a new vision *before* asking for the Spirit's guidance. *He* needs to be first in our hearts and minds. Otherwise, we achieve nothing. The Lord is our leader and our guide, not the other way around! He does not fit into our plans, but He intends that we fit into His. The Lord responds to our faith and to hearts that turn and seek Him.

Thought for the Day

The Lord said to Abram, "Leave your country, your people and your father's household and go to the land I will show you." ... So Abram left, as the LORD had told him; and Lot went with him.

—GENESIS 12:1, 4

WAIT A MINUTE

Abraham was not disobedient to the voice of the Lord. He listened to Him clearly, every word He said, and obeyed and went. He responded to God's call for deep commitment and performed actions that were intended by God. It is difficult to involve God in our decisions. I remember someone taking a decision to leave their life of ministry for a job with higher pay. It seemed that all the motivation for leaving stemmed from a desire for more material wealth and status. It was apparent that little prayer had gone into making the decision and little advice was sought. How contradictory to Abram's behavior!

The Spirit of God wants us to submit all our plans to Him. He wants to anoint us to do His will, and He wants His will to be first in our plans. He desires that we respond to His call and act in obedience, not to give up halfway or not even begin a life of service. Steps in faith result in witnessing God move in power through us. The challenge is great, but the life gained from it is incomparable in its fullness.

QUESTIONS TO CONTEMPLATE

1. In what unexpected ways have you known God to respond to your needs or those of others?

2. Do you allow Him to lead and reveal things by His Spirit rather than assuming that He will work to your agenda?

SPACE TO REFLECT

Ask God to increase our faith to see the lives of many people being healed and transformed. How far do we live in obedience simply asking that God would not just bless our activities for our lives but govern all our plans for the future?

A TIME TO PRAY

Father, help me to have right expectations of You and Your work. Forgive me for assuming that You will work to my agenda. Help me to hear Your will more clearly in the future and always look to follow that first. Amen.

THE RENEWAL:
RECEIVING THE SPIRIT

THE TWENTIETH CENTURY was labeled as "the era of the Holy Spirit," and a new emphasis had come on the need to "know God." People became more hungry for God and more reluctant to accept that the answer to their questions might lie in a stereotypical process. Many desired to know God in a deeper and more intimate way. Many desired to be filled with His Holy Spirit. The question was, how?

We need to be willing to have Him meet us and engage in our need by whatever means He chooses. Our own collaboration with His will and purpose for us takes place when we begin to ask the Lord Jesus to fill us with His Holy Spirit.

If He then assures you in your heart that He has done that already, just keep going on with Him! If He does not give you that assurance, then:

1. Present yourself—Romans 12:1–2
2. Ask—Luke 11:9–11
3. Obey—Acts 5:32
4. Have faith—Galatians 3:2

If you then still feel uncertain or unclear, do not hesitate to go to a mature Christian who can help. We do not have to feel that everything has to happen for us alone; after all, the Lord has given us to be a mutual support to one another. We do need to remember that Paul had to wait for Ananias to come and lay hands on him. We may need to receive laying on of hands ourselves as the visible, external sign that the living God is at work within us.

VACANT ROOMS

You could say that each one of us is like a hotel full of many different rooms, one for each aspect of our lives. The Spirit's desire is to empty each room of the garbage that is in there. He wants to clean the rooms completely and then move in to inhabit them. The difficulty is that we want to limit the areas of our lives in which the Spirit is allowed to rule and to reign. We often try to confine our Lord to one room, and that will never be sufficient.

The Spirit of God is calling on us to surrender our lives *totally* to Him. Without the Spirit, we will combat nothing, and closed off rooms in our hearts will remain. But with Him we can open each door one by one, allowing Him to come in and fill us completely. Ultimately this process will equip us to reflect Jesus more and more to the people that we meet. For too long we have hidden in fear from that simple but basic and life-transforming thing that God wants to do within each one of us.

If we are to see a major move of God in our nation, then that work will begin in individual lives. If we are to challenge our society with the good news of the Jesus they reject, then we must discover a new power from outside ourselves. The source of that power lies within God Himself. The Holy Spirit lies at the very heart of our mission. He is the "helper" whom God has given to us. He is our guide who not only points out the direction for us to go, but also He actually wants to take us there.

There is a danger that, because we know these truths so well, we might find that our very "familiarity could breed contempt." We must never forget that the One who indwells our lives is no less than the Holy Spirit of the living God. We should always remember that Jesus sternly forbade sinning against His Spirit, and the apostle Paul warned us of the danger of grieving the Holy Spirit.

One could almost imagine Paul raising his index finger as he admonished the church in Thessalonica, "Do not put out the Spirit's fire" (1 Thess. 5:19). We need to heed that same warning for today and let it burn!

To some of us the call will come simply to humble ourselves and pray; others will need to seek ministry and help. The end result must be the same—lives filled and renewed by the Spirit of God. Then, and only then, will people recognize what they saw in those early disciples—the life of Jesus reflected in His people. For that is the reason why the Holy Spirit has been given, not to point in His own direction but to draw the attention of everyone who is prepared to look toward Jesus.

THOUGHT FOR THE DAY

Therefore I urge you brothers, in view of God's mercy, to offer your bodies as living sacrifices, holy and pleasing to God—this is your spiritual act of worship.

—ROMANS 12:1

WAIT A MINUTE

We all know that God wants His people to be filled with the Holy Spirit. He doesn't want us to determine how He is going to fill us, but rather He wants us to submit ourselves to His direction and leading because He knows best!

All the Holy Spirit ever desires is to reveal more of Jesus to us, in us, and through us. So ask the Lord to fill you with His Spirit. If He assures you that He has done that already—then keep going!

Remember:

- Present yourself (Rom. 12:1–2)
- Ask (Luke 11:9–11)
- Obey (Acts 5:32)
- Have faith (Gal. 3:2)

QUESTIONS TO CONTEMPLATE

1. Are you afraid of what might happen if you ask Jesus to fill you with His Spirit?

2. What are you afraid of? (Write down your thoughts and feelings about this.)

SPACE TO REFLECT

Offer each one of your thoughts and fears to God. Allow Him to assure you that He is one to be trusted and is at work even if you do not feel anything immediately. Be careful that once you have allowed the Spirit to fill the rooms in your life that He is never shut out again.

A TIME TO PRAY

Lord, I so want to give myself again to You. Please will You send Your Spirit to come into every area of my life and to cleanse those parts that I have tried to keep shut off from You? Spirit of God, give me the strength not to just halfway open the door but to let You in completely. Right now would You come and fill me with Your Holy Spirit, and give me the faith to believe that You have done so? Amen.

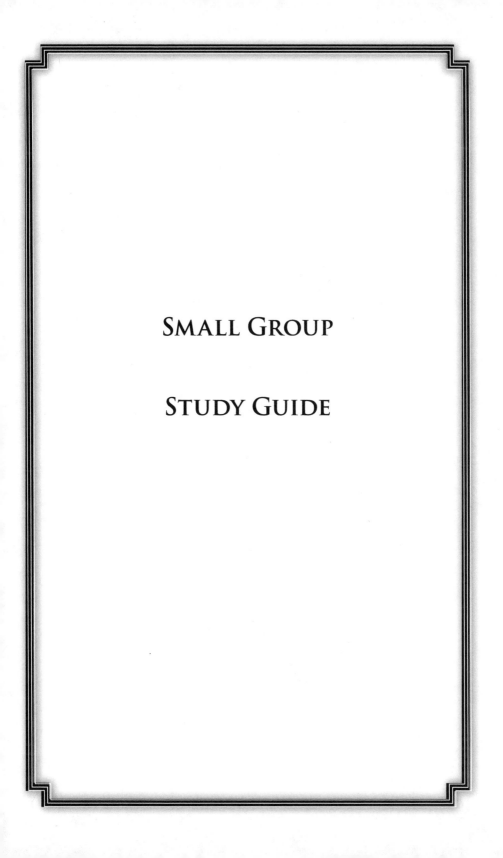

SMALL GROUP

STUDY GUIDE

Unpacking the Material

*T*HE MATERIAL THAT now follows is designed as a series for small group discussion. The intention is to help us to receive all that God wants to say to us through *Alive in the Spirit*. We may strongly believe that the Lord wants to transform our ministries, to make us wonderfully effective for Him. But in order to do this He wants us to grapple with our understanding of the Holy Spirit with one another. The Father's heart is to equip each one of us individually and as a body to recognize the importance of His Spirit's work in our lives.

In the next seven sessions we will seek to deepen our knowledge and love of God. There will be a strong theme headlining each of the weekly sessions to link directly with the daily meditations for the appropriate week. Each week the theme will be unpacked for discussion and a significant variety of questions are asked to help us explore each theme more fully. Then there is the opportunity to take things further with suggestions and questions to help us all implement important life changes in the week ahead.

Ultimately, our prayer must be that the Holy Spirit will be given that place in each one of our lives that He desires so that we may come to know the power of the Holy Spirit at work in our lives in ways that we have never really known before. It is the Spirit Himself who possesses the power and authority to make this dream come true.

Suggested Format

Some background information is provided to enable us to see how these sessions have been put together and, therefore, to help every leader to extract the maximum benefit from each session for the leader and for each group member. Each session is laid out as follows:

Title and Theme (suggested time allotment—3–4 minutes): This is based on the weekly material. For instance, session 2 serves to amplify the individual studies that make up week 2. This session will focus on how the Spirit of God leads and directs His people. So this can simply be announced at the beginning of the session. The theme provides the underlying thought that will permeate the entire session and enables the group to understand in which direction they should be going.

Summary (suggested time allotment—5 minutes): It is worth reading the summary (or perhaps asking someone from the group to read it) to benefit those who have not been doing the individual studies. It will provide a refresher in order to aid the ensuing discussion. If you have the impression that some have not read the daily entries, encourage them to do so. Reading the material during the week will help the discussion to go deeper and ultimately help everyone to gain more from the sessions.

Icebreaker (suggested time allotment—5 minutes): You may choose to do the icebreaker at this point, earlier in the meeting, or skip it altogether. Whatever you decide, don't spend too much time on this activity so that it doesn't drag on. The purpose is to make people feel relaxed enough to share with the person sitting next to them, so that they find it easier to share with the entire group.

Going Deeper (suggested time allotment—25–35 minutes): These questions are really the heart of the session and therefore the area that will require the most time. Discuss these together.

Taking It Further (suggested time allotment—15 minutes): At the leader's discretion, these additional thoughts can be discussed in the session or taken home for further individual reflection.

Pause to Pray: You may have noticed we did not place a suggested time limit on this part of the session. As you pray, be sensitive to the move of the Holy Spirit among the group members. As the discussion draws to a close, offer people the chance to sit quietly for a few minutes to digest all that has been said. Suggest that they allow the Lord to show them what He wishes to imprint on their minds and hearts from the session. Then ask the group if there is anything particular that has really spoken to them so that these things can be prayed through together. Finally, use the last point as a focus for prayer. The leader may also wish to end the study with a closing prayer.

SOME FINAL SUGGESTIONS FOR THE GROUP LEADER

Prior to your first study session, it might be helpful to share a meal together. This will help people to come prepared to be more vulnerable with each other. At this initial meeting it might be helpful to share the following:

1. The reason for meeting together. Clarify the need for trust within the group. Anything shared during the discussion is at the individuals' discretion and remains confidential.

2. Discuss the session format that you intend to use. We have provided suggested time allotments for each session format, *but these are guidelines.* As the leader, you, along with the group members, can decide what works best for all.

3. Decide on an ideal length of time to meet, the dates, and group expectations.

4. Remind everyone to bring a Bible!

5. Encourage each person to do the daily individual material prior to the next session. This way they will come prepared.

Know your group. Being ignorant of their backgrounds and strong character traits may limit your discussion. Getting to know your group from the beginning will facilitate deeper interaction. The same will often apply to group members keeping in touch with each other.

If someone wishes to discuss an issue for longer than the time allowed, then quietly ascertain if there are others in the group who feel the same way or whether the general feeling is that it is time to move on. Remember that as the group leader, you do have the final say. Get involved with the discussion, but also be ready to step back and allow others to run with it.

If you are struggling to get the discussion going and have already given some time for response, either share some of your own opinions or alter the question slightly to arouse a reaction from people.

A Closing Thought

Remain accountable to one another. You may not have the assurance that you truly are filled, or being filled, with the Holy Spirit. The best thing is to continue talking with someone after these sessions have finished. Don't become content with where you are or become in danger of putting out the Spirit's fire, but rather keep on encouraging it! Be wary of living in past experiences, such as conversion or another time of "Spirit filling." Remember Ephesians 5:18, which literally translated means "continue being filled with the Spirit."

WEEK 1:
WHERE WOULD WE BE
WITHOUT THE SPIRIT?

Session 1

Title: Where Would We Be Without the Spirit?

Theme: *"The sad truth is that during long periods of Christian history, the Holy Spirit has more often been regarded as a silent partner, the forgotten member of the Trinity."* We are asking today: Without the Spirit of God where would we be? Is He a silent partner, and therefore would His absence make any difference to our church life?

SUMMARY

All of us need to be drawn back again to be reminded and to understand afresh the fullness and truthfulness of the Trinity—to help us to see the 3-in-1, as the Godhead truly is. Max Anders in *FAQ's About the Holy Spirit,* says that "many people see God, in the Trinity, as a 'He,' a 'He,' and an 'it.'" But we must accept that the Holy Spirit is by no means an "it!" He is a "He," equally a part of and, therefore, on equal footing with the other two Persons of the Godhead.

The challenge we face is to consider what life without the Spirit of God would really look like. We need to ask ourselves the important question of whether the power and significance of the Holy Spirit has been watered down or even lost in our churches. Have our fear, doubt, and suspicion resulted in us putting reins on the Spirit, preventing His power from transforming lives?

Ultimately the Bible is clear that the present activity of the Holy Spirit in each of our lives is absolutely vital to all of our church ministry. It is not the Father, Son, and *Holy Scripture*, but the Father, Son, *and Holy Spirit* whom we worship. We are completely lost without the power of the Spirit, and our service for Jesus becomes obsolete without Him. "It is to the Church that God has given the New Testament message of salvation and it is by the power of the Spirit that the Church takes that message to the ends of the earth."

ICEBREAKER

Ask the person sitting next to you these questions:

1. Which "Person" of the Trinity is most spoken about in your church? Why? (For example, there's greater emphasis on God the Father than on the God the Holy Spirit.)

2. Why do you think the other Person(s) in the Godhead are not discussed as much?

GOING DEEPER

1. If the Holy Spirit were to be taken out of your church today, what difference would there be?

2. Day 3 suggested that Christians generally find it easier to understand and relate to God the Father and God the Son, but they find it much harder to grasp the concept of God the Holy Spirit. Discuss this together, and see who agrees and who disagrees.

3. Read 2 Timothy 1:7. Are the three characteristics of the Spirit listed in this scripture alive in the church today? Why or why not?

4. Think of a circumstance in which the Holy Spirit's manifest presence was so real to you. What happened to cause you to become more aware of His presence?

5. In Matthew 28:19 Jesus tells the disciples to "go and make disciples of all nations, baptizing them in the name of the Father, and of the Son, and of the Holy Spirit." He knows that the Father and the Spirit are as equal as Himself. If these are God's words, why do we find it hard to give the Lord's Spirit this same affirmation?

TAKING IT FURTHER

Jesus said, "And I will ask the Father, and he will give you another Counselor to be with you forever—the Spirit of truth" (John 14:16–17). The Spirit has been sent to us to dwell within us and to work through us.

How might we allow the Spirit of God room to move in our churches?

What changes do we need to make in our own lives so that the Spirit's work can come into all the fullness that God intended for each one of us?

PAUSE TO PRAY

Are there any key thoughts emerging from the discussion? If so, pray through them together.

Pray that we would give the Holy Spirit His rightful place in our lives. What will it take in terms of change if, this month, He is to be viewed as more than just a "silent partner"?

WEEK 2:
The Holy Spirit: God's Map Book

Session 2
    Title: The Holy Spirit: God's Map Book
    Theme: God's desire is to direct His people through each day of their lives. It is His heart that we surrender ourselves completely to His divine purposes that we may become the very hands and feet of Jesus.

SUMMARY

We are called to realize that the Spirit of God is active in our individual lives today. We cannot just know *about* Him; we need to accept that He *dwells within us* and works through us in power and authority!

God longs to guide His people, and His Spirit is the unique way in which He does this (John 16:13). There are multitudes of ways that we receive His guidance: through circumstances, Scripture, other people, and dreams (Acts 16:9), but each one requires testing. It is also interesting how God works. He often places us in situations where we had no intention of being and at a time when we least expect to suit His divine purposes.

We are called to come under the authority of Jesus Christ, allowing His Spirit to determine our actions and behavior. Paul strongly states in Romans that "those who live according to the sinful nature have their minds set on what that nature desires, but those who live in accordance with the Spirit have their minds set on what the Spirit desires" (Rom. 8:5).

We might have an idea of the place where God wants us to be, but getting there can be a real challenge. Thankfully the Spirit of God not only guides us, but He also helps us to arrive at our destination. He is a personal friend and advocate ready to make our defense and to help us with daily decisions.

ICEBREAKER

Share with the group a time when you went on a trip and got lost. Who was with you? Where were you going? When did you realize you were lost? How did you find your way to your final destination? What did you use to get there?

GOING DEEPER

1. Jesus' strong words of direction in the upper room included "peace be with you" (John 20:19). These were key words that the disciples were privy to more than once. Why do you think they were so important? Are they still so today?

2. The Gospel of John refers to the Holy Spirit as a helper (to assist us), counselor (to guide us), comforter (to console us), and advocate (to plead our case). Have you known the Spirit to work in *all* these ways or just one or two? (Ask four volunteers to share examples from their experience to cover each attribute.)

3. "He (the Holy Spirit) gave people visions and dreams (Acts 10:1–20) and revealed prophecies and scripture as he guided the authors of the New Testament (2 Pet. 1:21; 3:15–16; 2 Tim. 3:16–17)."[1] The Holy Spirit was powerfully living and active in the New Testament. Where do we see evidence that He is living and active today? Give examples.

4. The Lord will often put us in situations where we had no intention of being and at a time when we least expect, to suit His divine purposes. Has anyone in the group had this happen to them? Encourage a brief sharing of experiences.

5. Too often Christians try to find God through their own intellect, to respond to Him with their own emotions, and to serve Him as an act of their own will. What is the problem with doing that? What needs to change?

TAKING IT FURTHER

Read Galatians 3:3–5.

Paul is addressing the Galatians because he recognizes the importance of living by the Spirit of God and is desperate to see them live that way.

Are we also, in our own lives, caring too much about attaining our goal by human effort? Have we somehow lost our focus and forgot to surrender to Him? (If there is time, and a level of trust has been established within the group, these questions can be discussed during the session. If not, then encourage members to read them on their own later.)

This week allow the Spirit of God to take control of each life afresh, daily yielding to His authority and laying down each "well-intentioned activity" to Him, thus giving the Spirit access to focus the mind, will, and emotions of every one of us and in the best possible way.

PAUSE TO PRAY

Explore if there are any key thoughts emerging from the discussion. If so, encourage the group to pray them through together.

Pray together that the Holy Spirit will have fresh authority in our lives this week as we daily surrender ourselves entirely to Him.

WEEK 3:
The Fight of Our Lives

Session 3

    Title: The Fight of Our Lives

    Theme: Living in today's world can be a dangerous business! If we are going to follow God seriously, allowing the Spirit to be a vibrant active person in our lives, then we also have to acknowledge that we are engaged in a spiritual battle. Whatever the enemy tries to do to destroy our lives and ministries, he cannot defeat us in our mission. We can rest assured that Christ has had the ultimate victory through His work on the cross. If we are living in the power of the Spirit of Christ, we can fight the devil's attacks head on, gaining ground for the kingdom of God.

SUMMARY

We are engaged in a real battle, with a real enemy, and without the Spirit we are ill-equipped to fight. We need to recognize some of the devil's tactics and allow the light of the Spirit of God to expose his dark deeds. The good news is that Satan is limited in his power—he is temporary and localized. Unlike the Holy Spirit, he cannot be in more than one place at one time, without an army of powers to help him. He will try to tempt us to be self-indulgent by offering us all the things of this world that are merely temporary and contrary to the Spirit's eternal will for our lives. The enemy wants us to step out of the Father's will because He knows that it will destroy us, yet the Spirit longs that we soak ourselves in the truth of God's Word so that He can lead us and guide us into all truth.

If we are to overcome the enemy, then we need the full armor of God (Eph. 6:13), and we need to pray effectively in the Spirit as often as we can (Eph. 6:18). Nothing is a more appropriate defense, and our prayer acts as a launch pad to help to change the state of things on earth.

ICEBREAKER

When was the last time you felt as if you were in "the heat of the battle"? What were the circumstances? How did you get through that difficult time?

GOING DEEPER

1. "While my mind tends to revolt against the idea of a God of love acting as the author of suffering, I do believe that He permits His enemy to throw it at us at times" (Day 15). Discuss this excerpt together.

2. "It is not when life is easy, but rather when we are going through difficult times, that God will often choose to speak directly to us....It is...while we are enduring an arid wilderness experience that God demonstrates to us...His victory over the enemy" (Day 15). When was the last time you experienced a similar situation? Allow those who are willing the opportunity to share their own illustration, or that of (anonymously) someone they know.

3. Our Western world has become so materially developed and hedonistic that we have somehow managed to separate the spiritual and the secular. We are not quick to look for spiritual answers, often assuming mechanics or science is the reason behind the problem. In what ways can we combat this and introduce people to the real spiritual truth of Jesus when they appear "not to need Him"?

4. Instead of coming under God's authority, Israel failed in their response to temptation and ended up taking forty years to complete a two-week journey. How could they have overcome the temptations thrown their way and broken the cycle that they were encompassed in?

5. Read Ephesians 6:18. In what new ways could the church engage in effective prayer to come against the enemies' tactics?

TAKING IT FURTHER

Jesus was tempted by the devil in the desert (Luke 4). The devil tries to tempt us in similar ways. The enemy offers us anything to keep us self-indulgent and complacent (turn stones into bread). He offers us "the kingdoms of the world" to sell us temporary earthly dreams. And finally, the devil asks us to step outside the Father's will and to trust *him* (throw ourselves down to be rescued by angels).

(If there is time, and a level of trust has been established within the group, the following questions can be discussed during the session. If not, then encourage members to read them on their own later.)

☞ In what ways can we limit our self-indulgence and complacency?

☞ How can we better "live in the light of His coming" rather than filling our lives with earthly things?

☞ How can we stay faithful to our Father's will without giving in to the devil's schemes?

PAUSE TO PRAY

Are there any key thoughts emerging from the discussion? If so, pray through them together.

Pray together that each will recognize that we are engaged in spiritual battle but that Christ has given us the victory over Satan's attacks.

WEEK 4:
Supernatural Living

Session 4

    Title: Supernatural Living

    Theme: The Lord doesn't desire us to have a distant impersonal understanding of His Holy Spirit at work in our lives. His heart is for us to know and accept Him not only as a daily living reality at work in us, but also as a powerful person equipping us for action.

SUMMARY

The Holy Spirit wants to fill our lives in such a powerful way that we are prepared for supernatural living. His desire is for each one of us to realize that He can and will guide us into all truth. The Spirit's aim is for us to live in this truth and not just to believe it.

John the Baptist acknowledged that the Spirit was a vibrant, powerful reality for all believers (Matt 3:11). He knew that the fire of God's Spirit could come and burn up the old, giving us new life and transforming us more into Christ's likeness.

The Holy Spirit was at work in the early believers and is still at work in the lives of believers today. He wants to equip us to share the love of Christ in an effective and authentic way. The Spirit compels us to share the truth that we have found, not just through preaching but also through compassionate actions and a demonstration of the Spirit's power. This way we will be lights in the world that will illuminate the darkness and move toward a glorious future with Christ in eternity. Living in our future hope and refusing to be caught in the worries of tomorrow will better enable us to grasp the reality of what lies ahead (Rev. 21:4).

ICEBREAKER

Find someone in the group with whom you feel comfortable to do this exercise. Ask each other—on a scale of 1 to 10 with 1 being "I know about the Spirit impersonally, more as a vague force," and 10 being, "I know the Spirit personally, and He is a vibrant reality in my life"—where you would place yourself and why.

Going Deeper

1. Moses doubted his ability to share the message that God had given to him, despite the Lord telling him that He would give him the words to say (Exod. 4:10–12). The Lord still promises His Holy Spirit to give His disciples the words to say (Luke 12:11–12). Why then do we still struggle to share His truth?

2. The Holy Spirit was at work in the early believers to promote compassionate actions (Acts 6:3), demonstrate spiritual power (Acts 6:8), and generate bold proclamations (Acts 7:52). When was the last time that you witnessed one, or all, of these aspects at work in someone's life? When was the last time you witnessed any, or all, of these aspects at work *in your own* life? If you have not experienced them, what do you think is holding you back? Share to encourage one another.

3. "To have social action without the gospel message would accomplish little more than the puny efforts of secular humanism. But taken the other way round, we are left with the barren emptiness of words without deeds" (Day 37). Does your church engage in both, and if so, is the right balance achieved? Discuss together.

4. Many Muslims who have come to Christ have been converted through dreams and visions. Words and works have not been sufficient, so wonders have taken place. Why do you think it is easy to acknowledge that these experiences happen in other countries, but somehow feel that "signs and wonders" don't happen as often in our own country? Explain.

5. Read Matthew 5:16. How can we let our lights shine in our world (drawing people to Jesus) without compromising our relationship with Him and our belief system?

Taking It Further

Read Romans 8:14–16.

Sometimes we forget the hope of eternity in our hearts and allow fear of the future to rule rather than faith in a God who has it all under control. The Holy Spirit is our hope of glory. (If there is time, and a level of trust has been established within the group, the following questions can be discussed during the session. If not, then encourage members to read them on their own later.)

    ☞ How can we live free from fear and more in the future hope awaiting us?

    ☞ If Jesus returned tomorrow, do you feel that your church is ready to meet Him face to face? Why or why not?

PAUSE TO PRAY

Are any key thoughts emerging from the discussion? If so, pray through them together.

Pray together that your church will be so demonstrably Spirit-filled that the world may recognize that something supernatural is happening. Ask for boldness and belief in your witness so that you might be able to affirm gratefully that your mission to the world is proving to be powerful and effective.

WEEK 5:
Gifts and Graces

Session 5
    Title: Gifts and Graces
    Leader's note: Print copies of gift list for the group (Day 29) prior to the session. You may also wish to print the three groupings of spiritual gifts (Day 34) for use in question 3.
    Theme: The Holy Spirit is a gift to us from God. The Spirit, in turn, gives good gifts to us, His spiritual children. His desire is that we recognize, accept, and use these gifts in order to give glory to God, to extend His kingdom, and to build one another up within the body of Christ.

Summary

We are all unique, individual parts of the body of Christ that are called to work together in harmony to make a difference in this world for the Lord. Unfortunately our fear, competitiveness, comparisons, and inability to realize our own potential can inhibit or even prevent us from properly receiving and using these gifts that God has graciously given to us.

Recognizing and using our gifts carries great responsibility. We must not use them for our own selfish purposes but rather to serve the Lord. They need to be handled carefully and developed under the authority of the local church. The Lord has not given us the gifts with the intention of taking them back—they are freely given in love. The gifts are not just our natural talents (which we all have) but anointed gifts that clearly identify the Spirit at work in our lives. All the gifts are important to God, and we should not place some higher than others. Nor should we be afraid of spiritual gifts because we don't fully understand them.

Some people would argue that we do not need these gifts because they shift our focus wrongly, or they are not as important as the fruit. However, Scripture is clear that these still can be relevant for Christians now and not just in the lives of the early believers. If we argue that these gifts are not valid, then we remove a powerful work of the Holy Spirit and can become guilty of reducing Christianity to the level of an alternative philosophy, thus inviting Satan's supernatural influence to fascinate society instead.

ICEBREAKER

(Use the ministry gift list from Day 29.) With someone whom you know relatively well, spend a short time identifying the gifts that you believe he or she has. Suggest ways that he or she could use them. Share together with the purpose of encouraging and building each other up.

GOING DEEPER

1. Does our church encourage (or discourage) people to recognize their spiritual gifts and to use them under the authority of the leadership? In what situations have you seen this happen? Discuss.

2. Review the three primary objections given to the use of the gifts of the Spirit today (Day 35). Which of these objections, if any, exist in our church? What reasoning is behind the objection? How can we become more open to the gifts of the Spirit?

3. Consider the three groupings of spiritual gifts *(you may wish to print these out for the group from Day 34):*

    Gifts of revelation (the power to know): discerning of spirits, word of wisdom, and word of knowledge.
    Gifts of activity (the power to do): gift of healing, working of miracles, and gift of faith.
    Gifts for communication (the power to say): gift of tongues, interpretation, and prophecy.

    Is one of the three groupings more active in your church community? Which is the least used area? What would you like to see encouraged more?

4. Day 33 emphasized the "practice" of the gifts of the Spirit. What is the most effective way to use the gifts God has given you? If you're not operating in the gifts God gave you, then what do you think is stopping you?

5. First Corinthians 12 talks about the importance of spiritual gifts, emphasizing the gifts unique to us as individuals, and all regarded as valuable as one another. Verses 22–23 say, "On the contrary, those parts of the body that seem to be weaker are indispensable, and

the parts that we think are less honorable we treat with special honor." How can we actively value peoples gifts equally—treating those who are less honorable with greater honor?

Taking It Further

If we ignore the spiritual gifts, we remove the supernatural ingredient from Christianity, giving an open invitation to Satan to fascinate society by his own subtle but completely inferior tricks. We can also reduce Christianity to the status of an alternative philosophy.

(If there is time, and a level of trust already built within the group, some or all of the following questions can be discussed during the session. If not, then encourage members to read them on their own later.)

☞ Are we in danger of removing the supernatural ingredient from our own lives and the life of the church?

☞ Two hundred years ago John Wesley's concern was that the love of many was "waxed cold." Are we in danger of that today?

☞ Are we reducing Christianity, making it less than it should be? Or are we demythologizing it of false attitudes and practices? What needs to change?

Pause to Pray

Are there any key thoughts emerging from discussion? Pray through them together.

Pray together that the Lord would reveal the importance of spiritual gifts to each one of us, showing us where our gifts lie and the best ways that we can use them for Him.

WEEK 6:
Spirit-Filled Churches

Session 6

Title: Spirit-Filled Churches

Theme: The Lord does not plan for us to step outside of our houses and minister in our own strength; His desire is for the Holy Spirit to breathe power through the church, enabling us to complete the work and will of our Father. We are filled with the Spirit of God to enable our lives to reflect Jesus more and more. God's desire is for our lives to be an act of worship, so in all we say and do, we seek to give the glory back to Him.

SUMMARY

The dramatic growth of the early church was not achieved by men and women proclaiming the gospel in their own strength. The rapid transformation and spread of the church of our Lord was due to the Spirit of God equipping men and women to witness in power and authority (Acts 1:8). We cannot make a difference for the Lord in America or anywhere else in the world without the Holy Spirit to supernaturally empower us.

He does not deal with us just as individuals but also as a corporate whole. On the Day of Pentecost *all* the believers received the power of the Holy Spirit, thus enabling them to know God in an active and intimate relationship. The Spirit empowered the new community for its mission: equipping the church for its ministry.

Jesus' desire was that all His disciples "might be one" (John 17), serving out of love for one another. The church—then and now—is not made up of African Christians or American Christians. It is the body of Christ. We do not find our identity in our church buildings but in being the people of God. We are called to demonstrate that we are part of a universal church through loving and serving those who are poor, weak, and disadvantaged around the world.

There may be people who say that America is spiritually weak today, that we should give up because disaster looms just around the corner, or even that our time to share the truth is running out. Whatever the truth of our nation's spiritual state, we can hold on to the fact that Jesus has still given us His Spirit to make a radical difference today (Acts 2:18).

ICEBREAKER

Discuss the following question with someone next to you: What does worship mean to you?

GOING DEEPER

1. Some people regard the spiritual condition of America as desperately weak and spiritually poor; some predict that disaster is around the corner. There are those who say time is running out, and still others who fear that little hope is left. Discuss together.

2. "It is a sobering question to face honestly, but if the lifestyle of the Jerusalem church represents what the Holy Spirit does in the life of a local church, then how would we rate ourselves?…Or have we stopped short, stuck somewhere between the realities of Calvary and a genuine Pentecost?" (Day 37). Discuss this comment as a group.

3. Jesus' heart cry to His Father in John 17:21 was that His disciples "might be one"—loving and supporting each other to ensure the churches' survival. Do you consider your church to be "one in Christ Jesus?" (Gal. 3:28). In what ways could your church be more loving and supportive of each other?

4. "All were worshiping God in their own way. Some offered their hearts and lives to the Lord in a quiet meditative fashion; others expressed their sense of joy and gratitude with total abandon" (Day 38). Should there be more uniformity or greater diversity in the way that people worship in our church? Or should we expect to see people worshiping in lots of different ways? Why do you think that is?

5. The Holy Spirit gives us power, not just for ourselves but so we can serve others. How far does our generosity stretch—has it arrived overseas yet to the poor and disadvantaged? In what ways? Is there anything else that could be done?

TAKING IT FURTHER

Read Matthew 6:33. (If there is time, and a level of trust already built within the group, some or all of the following questions can be discussed during the session. If not, then encourage members to read them on their own later.)

1. What is your quest for?

2. Do you feel that your corporate hunger and thirst is for spiritual or material gain?

3. Is there a consensus within the church to seek His kingdom and righteousness above anything else?

4. In what ways do you think God is calling for change (if He is)?

PAUSE TO PRAY

Are there any key thoughts emerging from the discussion? Pray through them together.

Pray together that the Lord would renew and reenergize you for His work to witness to His truth in a dying world and to help you to live lives of true worship to Him.

WEEK 7:
LIVING BY THE SPIRIT

Session 7

   Title: Living by the Spirit

   Theme: What are we anointed for? The Holy Spirit has filled us and anointed us to receive blessings, healings, and deliverance; to endure sufferings; and to share the good news. The Holy Spirit wants to do more in our lives than what a one-time experience would achieve. We need the power of God daily to enable us to achieve what we never could alone. Ultimately the Lord's heart is that the indwelling Spirit in our lives will draw people to Jesus.

SUMMARY

Some people struggle with the concept of the Holy Spirit coming "upon" them and daily dwelling "within" them at the same time. It is not a rigid concept; He permanently lives in us and anoints our lives for particular acts of service. (Read about Samson in Judges 13:25; 14:6, 19; 15:4.) We need the infilling and the anointing of the Spirit to achieve our greatest potential in Christ Jesus. We must not be content with what we are, thinking that we have arrived. Instead, we need to continually submit our lives entirely to the direction of the Holy Spirit, letting our minds, emotions, and wills be controlled by Him. We each need to give God freedom to rule and reign in every area of our lives and not confine Him to certain parts. If we really are to see a work of God in our land, we must welcome the unique work of the Spirit in our individual lives and be careful not to "put out the Spirit's fire" (1 Thess. 5:19).

The baptism in the Holy Spirit has also created great controversy throughout the centuries. In New Testament terms, "baptism in the Holy Spirit" is often associated with repentance and faith as part of the conversion process. Since then, those Christians who have come to a deeper experience of the Spirit after conversion also refer to this as "baptism in the Holy Spirit." Because we use the same words in different ways, we often misunderstand each other. Despite these differences in opinion, we must be very careful not to insist that everyone follow the exact same spiritual path or that our understanding of the Spirit is superior to anyone else's. The living God is perfectly able to lead His people by different routes to the same destination. We can make very dangerous assumptions that result in us placing God's intentions in a narrow box and limiting Him.

Thankfully, we do agree that we all need the power of God in our lives and that each one of us receives the Spirit at conversion. The power will transform our ministries and us and move people closer to Jesus. Some of us will be called to humble ourselves and pray, while others will need to seek ministry and help to experience the Spirit's renewing day by day. Whatever it takes, we should do it, if we really are desperate to see people come face to face with our Lord.

ICEBREAKER

Ask the person next to you this question: Are you someone who pleads for a deeper experience from God since you gave your life to Christ, or do you feel satisfied that you received all that you needed at your point of conversion?

GOING DEEPER

1. D. L. Moody made a promise to God shortly after conversion to not allow twenty-four hours to pass without sharing Jesus. God doesn't demand this, but He does honor our efforts. Think for a moment. When was the last time you spoke to someone about the Lord? Share with someone in the group an individual who is on your heart for Christ's love to transform.

2. In regards to dealing with demonic presence in peoples' lives, there are six conditions for freedom to take place: humility, honesty, confession of sin, repentance, forgiveness of all others, and calling on the name of the Lord. Have you had experience with delivering people from demons? Share together. Have all these conditions (above) happened during the process of the individuals being set free?

3. John 15:13 says, "Greater love has no one than this; that he lay down his life for his friends." These words of Jesus remind us that we should be prepared to suffer for the sake of others. Do you think that the idea of suffering is a foreign concept to most Christians, especially in America? Why is that?

4. Read Matthew 11:5. It is clear that Jesus has anointed His followers to heal. Have you had any experiences of

healing people or seeing people receive healing? Have you personally ever received healing? Why do you think we don't see more of it?

5. One preacher commented that "the average spiritual temperature in the church is so low that when a healthy man comes along, everyone thinks that he has a fever." Have you seen evidence of this in your church? Do you think that your church is "missing out on the Spirit of Pentecost" in any way?

TAKING IT FURTHER

First Thessalonians 5:19 says, "Do not put out the Spirit's fire." (If there is time, and a level of trust within the group, some the following questions can be discussed during the session. If not, then encourage members to read them on their own later.)

1. As a nation, do you think that we are in danger of putting this fire out? Why?

2. Have we given the Spirit freedom to move in our church so that the life of Jesus is reflected in us and therefore drawing people toward Him?

PAUSE TO PRAY

Are there any key thoughts emerging from discussion? Pray through them together.

Pray together that you will not miss out on all that the Holy Spirit desires to do in you and your church. As the early believers went out and changed their world following Pentecost, keep on asking God for a powerful move of His Spirit in the world, starting with you right now. Pray that, as a church, you will make a significant spiritual impact on the world's landscape, drawing many toward Jesus.

NOTES

DAY 4
THE POWER TO CHANGE THE WORLD

1. A. W. Tozer, *Gems From Tozer* (N.p.: Christian Publications, 1969); quoted in *Paths to Power* (Camphill, PA: Christian Publication, 1979).

DAY 14
THE HELPER: HE CAN MAKE A DIFFERENCE

1. A well-known saying of Tertullian, who lived in the midst of persecution. *Encyclopedia.com*, s.v. "Tertullian," http://www.encyclopedia.com/html/T/Tertulli.asp (accessed October 13, 2003).

2. Max Anders, *Just the FAQ*s About the Holy Spirit* (Nashville, TN: Thomas Nelson, 2002), 15.

DAY 16
THE TEMPTATIONS: DEFEATING THE ENEMY

1. A. W. Tozer, *Born After Midnight* (Camphill, PA: Christian Publications).

DAY 21
THE VICTORS: IN A TRIAL OF STRENGTH

1. "Stand Up, Stand Up for Jesus" by George Duffield Jr. Public domain.

DAY 31
THE PEDIGREE: AS IT WAS AT THE BEGINNING?

1. Quoted in Henry Bettenson, ed., *The Early Church Fathers* (Oxford, Oxford University Press, 1956).

DAY 33
THE PRACTICE: GIFTS AND HOW TO USE THEM

1. C. Peter Wagner, *Your Spiritual Gifts Can Help Your Church Grow* (Ventura, CA: Regal Books, 1994).

DAY 38
THE WORSHIP: A NEW DAY DAWNING

1. A. W. Tozer, *Worship: The Missing Jewel of the Evangelical Church* (Camp Hill, Penn: Christian Publications, 1996), 8–9; quoted in "Excerpts from A. W. Tozer," Messages From the Heart, http://www.heart-talks .com/truth27.html (accessed October 17, 2003).

DAY 39
THE MISSION: CHURCH BEYOND BORDERS

1. World Relief: Where We Work—Africa, Sudan, "Clive Calver Visits Sudan," http://www.wr.org/where_we_work/africa/sudan/calver_visits .asp (accessed October 17, 2003).

DAY 40
THE UNITY: WORKING TOGETHER IN GOD

1. Richard Baxter, *The Practical Works of Richard Baxter*, published in London in 1707.

DAY 41
THE ACTION: WAITING FOR GOD

1. Statistics based on the author's knowledge he obtained as the president of World Relief.

DAY 45
THE PROCLAMATION: ANOINTED TO WITNESS

1. R. A. Torrey, *Why God Used D. L. Moody* (N.p.: The Bible Institute Colportage Ass'n, 1923); quoted in Calver and Delve, *God Can Use You* (Marshalls, 1983).

DAY 48
THE FILLING: ANOINTED FOR RENEWAL

1. Clive Calver, *The Holy Spirit* (London: Scripture Union, 1984), 90.

SMALL GROUP STUDY GUIDE

WEEK 1
WHERE WOULD WE BE WITHOUT THE SPIRIT?

1. Anders, *Just the FAQ*s About the Holy Spirit*, 14.

WEEK 2
THE HOLY SPIRIT—GOD'S MAP BOOK

1. Anders, *Just the FAQ*s About the Holy Spirit*, 13.